Homestead Harmony: Off-Grid Projects for a Balanced Life

Create, Build, and Thrive Off the Beaten Path

Ava Davis

Table of Contents

INTRODUCTION

Welcome to "Homestead Harmony: Off-Grid Projects for a Balanced Life." This e-book is more than just a guide; it's your passport to a less ordinary life that embraces simplicity, self-sufficiency, and the allure of off-grid living. In a world constantly in a rush, this book is your compass, guiding you through projects, ideas, and practices that empower you to build a fulfilling life off the traditional grid. Our subtitle, "Create, Build, and Thrive Off the Beaten Path," encapsulates the essence of our shared adventure.

In the following pages, we will go on a homesteading journey, digging into the concepts, projects, and viewpoints that characterize a lifestyle that is off-grid and balanced. The homestead lifestyle is not only a movement; it is a philosophy that involves making a conscious decision to establish a connection with the land, engage in sustainable practices, and build a feeling of autonomy. If you are a seasoned homesteader or just beginning to dream of a life off the beaten road, this e-book is meant to inspire, enlighten, and lead you through the complexities of constructing your own hideaway in the woods. It is accessible to anybody interested in homesteading.

The chapters that are to come will reveal a rich tapestry of information, beginning with the basic idea of your farm and progressing down to the specifics of sustainable energy, water management, and shelter building. We will discuss the pleasures of cultivating your food, preparing meals without the need for electricity, and developing a harmonious and self-sufficient lifestyle. Along the process, you will learn how to balance technological advancements and the simplicity of living off the grid. This will ensure that your homestead is a place to relax and a vibrant community linked to one another.

The further we go into each chapter, the more you will discover helpful advice, do-it-yourself projects, and a wealth of material that will assist you in navigating the hurdles of homesteading and celebrating the victories you achieve. Whether your objective is to detach yourself from the craziness of the city, reduce the amount of damage you cause to the environment, or reestablish a connection with the natural world, "Homestead Harmony" is the company you need on this beautiful trip. Therefore, let us flip the page and start constructing a life that is in sync with the rhythm of the land, where the act of creating, growing, and thriving will become the cornerstones of your existence when you are not connected to the grid.

CHAPTER I

The Homestead Vision

Establishing Your Homestead Goals

Setting homestead objectives that are both specific and well-considered is the first and most crucial stage in the process of pursuing a lifestyle that is independent of the grid. This process entails visualizing the life you want to live, determining the reason for your homestead, and establishing attainable goals that align with your ideals and goals for the future. Living on a homestead goes beyond the traditional conventions of urban existence; it is a conscious decision to embrace self-sufficiency, sustainability, and a healthy interaction with our natural surroundings.

First things first, give some thought to the overall vision you have for your farm. How would you describe the perfect day spent on your family's property? What kind of relationship do you want to have with the land, the resources, and the people that live in the area around you? Creating a clear mental image will act as a beacon of light for you as you embark on your homesteading adventure. It might be a dream of growing your food, raising animals, or relying on sustainable energy sources to power your life. Your objectives for your homestead should reflect the unique combination of values, interests, and desires that define your vision for a life that is off of the grid and balanced.

Once the overarching vision has been developed, the next step is to break it down into more particular goals. Consider the practical features of your homestead, such as the property size, the kind of dwelling you want to construct, and the degree of self-sufficiency you wish to attain.

Are you imagining a garden run according to the principles of permaculture, an orchard, or possibly a successful animal husbandry operation? Outline the concrete actions that must be taken to transform these goals into a reality, keeping in mind that each objective may represent a different stage in your path toward being a proficient homesteader.

Regarding off-grid living, sustainability is frequently a fundamental component; therefore, it is necessary to incorporate environmentally friendly activities into your aims. This may entail the utilization of renewable energy sources such as solar or wind power, implementing water conservation technologies, or adopting sustainable construction principles. The goal-setting process ought to be a seamless integration of your aspirations with the principles of environmental stewardship. This will ensure that your homestead is a safe haven for you and an example of responsible living.

Financial concerns play a crucial part in establishing goals for a homestead. Create a budget that is both reasonable and comprehensive, taking into account the costs of land, the creation of infrastructure, and continuous maintenance. It is essential to think about how you will create revenue, whether it is through farming, artisanal skills, or other environmentally responsible methods. Setting goals that ensure your homestead can grow independently over the long term requires you to balance self-sufficiency and financial sustainability. This is an essential component of goal-setting.

Integration into the community is yet another essential component of homesteading objectives. It is crucial to choose the degree of social involvement you want on your farm, regardless of whether you want to use it as a lonely retreat or as a community that thrives off the grid. Give some thought to how your goals for your homestead might contribute to the community's overall well-being, therefore encouraging teamwork and shared values.

Due to the naturally dynamic nature of homesteading, flexibility is an essential component in goal-setting. As you acquire practical experience and get familiar with living off the grid, you should be willing to change your goals for yourself. The capacity to adjust one's behavior in response to shifting conditions, unanticipated obstacles, and newly discovered possibilities is a defining characteristic of successful homesteading. Recognize the importance of the learning curve and look at obstacles as chances for personal development and the improvement of your household objectives.

In conclusion, determining your homestead goals is the first and most crucial stage in transitioning to off-grid life. To do this, it is necessary to balance vision, practicability, sustainability, financial planning, and community participation. Your goals for your homestead will act as a compass that will lead you through the complex terrain of self-sufficiency and happy living. Through visualizing, expressing, and modifying your objectives, you may prepare the way for a homesteading experience that is in harmony with your most fundamental principles, establishing a sanctuary of equilibrium and purpose inside the embrace of the bounties of nature.

Designing Your Off-Grid Lifestyle

Designing an off-grid lifestyle takes careful planning and attention to detail; it's like drawing out a blueprint for a peaceful, satisfying, and sustainable way of life. The critical components of off-grid living are deliberate decisions that highly value environmental sustainability, self-sufficiency, and a close relationship with the natural world. In the process, you take on the roles of both resident and architect, influencing not just the outward layout of your farmstead but also its internal rhythms.

Choosing the ideal site is the first step in creating an off-grid existence. It includes more than just locating a gorgeous plot of land; it entails thoroughly assessing variables, including soil quality, climate, and local laws. Every geographic region has different possibilities and difficulties, and your chosen place will significantly impact how your homestead is designed. Whether tucked away on a sun-drenched hillside or in a wooded enclave, the setting serves as a blank canvas on which you may paint the picture of your off-grid existence.

Off-grid life depends heavily on energy; therefore, creating a sustainable energy system is essential. Popular options for producing energy off the grid include micro-hydro systems, wind turbines, and solar power. To provide a steady supply of electricity, the design should consider energy storage options in addition to accommodating the installation of these systems. A well-thought-out off-grid energy system minimizes environmental impact, encourages self-sufficiency, and lowers dependency on regular utilities.

Another crucial component of planning an off-grid existence is water management. Rainwater collection, effective storage strategies, and environmentally friendly watering techniques should all be included in the design. Water is a valuable resource that has to be handled carefully, and the homestead's layout should demonstrate a dedication to conservation. Careful water management fits with the more significant environmental responsibility mindset and enhances the sustainability of your off-grid living.

Your off-grid home's architecture is a canvas for both practicality and style. Natural ventilation, energy-efficient design, and sustainable construction materials should all be considered. Off-grid dwellings frequently follow small house living's maximization of space and reduction of environmental effects. The design must blend perfectly with the surroundings, making distinguishing between indoor and outdoor areas difficult and fostering a mutually beneficial interaction with the natural world.

A key component of off-grid life is food independence; therefore, when planning your farm, give room for gardening, orchards, and animal husbandry priority. Your garden's design may be informed by permaculture principles, which will increase soil fertility and encourage biodiversity. The aim is to develop a robust and fruitful food system that feeds your family and lessens its dependency on outside resources. The layout should make obtaining fresh, organic produce simple, establishing a close relationship with the food that powers your off-grid way of living.

Preserving food and cooking off the grid is essential to creating an independent existence. Solar ovens and rocket stoves are outdoor cooking options that may be easily included in your design. The design should also consider techniques for preserving food, such as root cellaring, canning, and drying. By having these components in the design, you honor the long-standing customs of sustainably preparing and storing food while improving the homestead's use.

Despite being frequently linked to urban living, technology has a role in off-grid design. Adopting technology that complies with sustainability guidelines is the problematic part. Off-grid houses may include energy-efficient technology, solar-powered appliances, and environmentally friendly devices. To create a harmonic synergy between technology and the off-grid ethos, the design should balance embracing contemporary life's advantages and reducing the ecological effect.

An off-grid existence requires self-care and wellness, and your homestead's layout should demonstrate your dedication to overall health. Set aside areas for rest, contemplation, and renewal. Include natural aspects in your design, such as expansive windows that showcase picturesque vistas or outdoor areas ideal for fitness and yoga. Off-grid living is about flourishing rather than just surviving, and the design should support a way of life that promotes mental and physical well-being.

One approach to incorporating creativity into your off-grid living is to create artisanal areas on your farm. Set aside space for woodworking, crafts, or any other artisanal skills you want to learn. With this design decision, your homestead becomes a space for creative expression and imaginative living in addition to practical life. You may add to the distinctiveness of your off-grid lifestyle and offer the opportunity to transform hobbies into sustainable activities by including handmade spaces.

Your off-grid existence should be designed with security and emergency readiness in mind. Storage for emergency supplies, easy access to dependable communication devices, and long-term security measures should all be included in the design. Planning for emergencies ensures your homestead is ready to face unforeseen difficulties and promotes flexibility and resilience.

The seasons and rhythms of your property should shape your off-grid existence. Accept that the seasons are cyclical and build your homestead to accommodate shifting weather patterns. On an off-grid farm, you should consider the ebb and flow of daily life and seasonal festivities and celebrations. The plan should be adaptable enough to consider how homesteading changes with the seasons.

To sum up, planning an off-grid lifestyle involves more than just the structure of your farm; it's a deliberate and comprehensive process. It entails imagining a sustainable, self-sufficient life and being in balance with the environment. Every element of your off-grid life, from choosing the ideal site to incorporating sustainable energy, water management, and food independence into the design, adds to the whole. Adopting deliberate design principles lays the groundwork for a life that resonates with balance, purpose, and the allure of off-grid living and creates a beautiful and valuable living area.

Balancing Self-Sufficiency and Modern Comforts

The quest for off-grid life is a challenging tango between the need for contemporary luxuries and self-sufficiency. This contrast is the foundation for a distinctive way of life that balances modern comforts with a desire for harmony with the natural world. Living off the grid, sometimes connected to a return to simplicity, raises an interesting question: How can one reconcile the need for contemporary conveniences that define comfort in the twenty-first century with the independent spirit of homesteading?

The intentionality of choosing is the fundamental component of this equilibrium. Living off the grid involves deliberately cutting ties with traditional electricity systems, water sources, and social conventions. The decision to create a self-sufficient lifestyle that honors the environment and revels in homesteading's independence was made on purpose. However, this independence does not mean giving up all contemporary conveniences. Instead, it forces people to reconsider and reframe what it means to be truly comfortable.

The energy sector is one main arena where this balance is negotiated. Using renewable energy sources, such as micro-hydro systems, wind turbines, or solar panels, is an example of the self-sufficiency of living off the grid. But the problem starts when one considers the variety of modern gadgets that are now a need in contemporary living. Energy usage must be carefully considered to maintain self-sufficiency while satisfying the need for contemporary amenities. It entails prioritizing energy-efficient appliances, forming thoughtful routines, and embracing a more purposeful way of living where energy is valued as a scarce resource that should be utilized sparingly.

Water is another essential component of off-grid life, which represents the delicate balance between contemporary comforts and self-sufficiency. Gathering rainwater and using sustainable irrigation techniques are necessary for the off-grid lifestyle. However, the comfort of having flowing water at the touch of a tap—a ubiquitous contemporary convenience—makes one reevaluate what is necessary. A balance is struck by combining water-saving techniques with creative ideas that preserve the convenience of a dependable water supply. Water, the lifeblood of off-grid living, becomes a dynamic interaction of old wisdom and modern technology to guarantee that both the demand for convenience and necessities are met.

Off-grid homes' architectural style perfectly perfectly balances modern luxuries and self-sufficiency. Tiny house living's eco-friendliness and simplicity align with sustainability and independence principles. But the problem comes when people consider incorporating contemporary conveniences like air conditioning, central heating, or other equipment that symbolize modern comfort. The answer is to use sustainable construction techniques emphasizing energy-efficient designs, passive heating and cooling, and natural insulation. This strategy allows off-grid living ideals and home comforts to live peacefully, resulting in a beautiful fusion of the two.

Food independence is a critical component of off-grid life, which offers a distinctive viewpoint on balancing contemporary luxuries and self-sufficiency. Growing one's food, whether in gardens, orchards, or livestock farming, is the essence of homesteading. However, the ease of grocery shopping and prepared foods challenges the idea of self-sufficiency. The balance is reached by adopting a hybrid strategy emphasizing organic, locally grown food while realizing that occasional reliance on outside resources upholds the fundamentals of off-grid life. It's a recognition that rare ease of modern food accessibility may coexist with self-sufficiency.

Off-grid cooking and preservation are another example of the complex compromises between modern luxuries and self-sufficiency. Off-grid living's independent spirit is well suited to outdoor cooking options like wood-fired stoves and solar ovens. However, there is a contradiction in the appeal of having a modern kitchen with all today's gadgets. The secret is to strike a balance between enjoying the contemporary convenience of a well-stocked kitchen on occasion and maintaining the taste of self- sufficiency by utilizing conventional food preservation techniques like canning, drying, or fermenting.

The interaction between self-sufficiency and contemporary amenities takes on an intriguing new dimension with technology in off-grid life. Off-grid households may want to become less dependent on the electrical grid. Still, eco-friendly devices, solar-powered appliances, and sustainable tech solutions all find a place in the world of technology. Adopting technology that aligns with environmental stewardship and sustainability ideals is a problem. The ease of contemporary technology may be carefully incorporated into off-grid life to improve comfort levels without sacrificing the goal of self-sufficiency.

As essential elements of off-grid life, wellness, and self-care offer a chance to rethink contemporary luxuries. Creating areas for rest, contemplation, and renewal reflects the self-awareness that comes with living off the grid. Embracing natural surroundings, outdoor areas, and mindfulness techniques replaces traditional concepts of comfort with a more profound, more meaningful well-being, even while contemporary spa amenities may be lacking.

Creating artisanal areas on the homestead allows for the integration of creativity into off-grid life. The usual function of artisanal skills is challenged by the need for contemporary conveniences, even when traditional craftsmanship is in line with self-sufficiency. Finding a balance involves setting aside areas for carpentry, crafts, or other artisanal abilities, encouraging a creative outlet while living off the grid. This integration gives a way to transform pastimes into sustainable activities and add to the homestead's distinctiveness.

Security and emergency readiness highlight the necessity of balancing contemporary luxuries and self-sufficiency.

Storage for emergency supplies, easy access to dependable communication devices, and long-term security measures should all be included in the design. A realistic and practical balance between contemporary requirements and self-sufficiency is ensured by acknowledging the occasional need to rely on modern tools for emergencies, even though self-reliance is the ultimate objective.

The seasonal fluctuations and the cyclical aspect of homesteading contribute an additional dimension to the intricate balance between self-reliance and contemporary conveniences. Off-grid living requires modifying daily patterns, accepting natural cycles, and responding to seasonal variations. Striking a balance means coordinating day-to-day operations with the cycles of nature, realizing that the essence of self-sufficiency is not in conflict with contemporary conveniences but rather in peaceful harmony with the natural world.

In conclusion, the art of off-grid life is striking a balance between contemporary conveniences and self-sufficiency. It necessitates making deliberate and deliberate decisions daily, balancing the independence of farming with the comforts of modern living. This careful balancing act between tradition and modernity is a sophisticated synthesis of the best elements from both cultures rather than a concession. Off-grid living turns into a canvas on which modern conveniences and sustainable ideas come together to create a way of life that is not just about surviving but thriving in a well-balanced mix of independence and convenience.

CHAPTER II

Setting Up Your Off-Grid Homestead

Choosing the Right Location

Setting up an off-grid homestead is a significant choice that requires excellent thought; choosing the appropriate site is the most crucial step in this process. Selecting a place for an off-grid project involves more than just picking a beautiful area; it takes into account a wide range of elements that will significantly influence its sustainability, self-sufficiency, and overall success.

The climate is one of the most important factors when deciding where to put an off-grid farm. A region's climate greatly influences the viability of some off-grid activities, like cultivating particular crops or using renewable energy sources. Planning and adjusting your farm operations to the natural rhythm of the environment requires a detailed awareness of the local climate, including temperature fluctuations, precipitation patterns, and seasonal changes.

Aside from climate, another important consideration that may significantly impact an off-grid farm's viability is the chosen site's soil condition. Planning a sustainable garden or orchard requires evaluating the soil's fertility, composition, and drainage potential. Your farm will thrive in harmony with the natural soil conditions if you do soil tests and understand the land's distinctive features. These findings will guide these decisions about crop selection, gardening techniques, and general land management.

Off-grid living places a high value on water quality and availability, so finding a spot close to a dependable water source is essential. Self-sufficiency requires having access to clean water for drinking, irrigation, and other household requirements. The presence of natural water sources, such as lakes, rivers, or wells, might influence the viability and sustainability of an off-grid farmhouse. Furthermore, appropriate water management requires understanding local laws, ordinances, and conservation techniques.

Legal issues and local laws are crucial when choosing a site for an off-grid homestead. Different regions have different zoning rules, construction requirements, and environmental regulations, which can significantly influence what off-grid activities you can use. To retain the liberty and self-sufficiency that come with off-grid living, you must conduct an in-depth study and comprehend the legal environment of your selected site.

An essential practical factor that might affect how well an off-grid farmhouse operates daily is accessibility. Being close to healthcare facilities, educational institutions, and necessary services may be vital to stay connected to the larger community. Evaluating the accessibility of supplies and the ease of movement to and from your homestead can help you lead a more robust and sustainable off-grid lifestyle.

Another factor to consider while choosing the ideal site for an off-grid homestead is the area's terrain. Specific tasks, like building structures, planting gardens, or using solar energy, may be more challenging to carry out on steep slopes, rocky terrain, or low-lying places. Comprehending the topography and inherent qualities of the terrain facilitates tactical arrangement that optimizes the utilization of accessible areas while reducing the ecological consequences of your off-grid pursuits.

Ecological concerns and biodiversity make your off-grid homestead healthier and more sustainable overall. Selecting a site that encourages a variety of plant and animal species helps maintain a healthy ecosystem and increases your homestead's resilience. Native plants and animals support natural pest management, soil fertility, and general ecological balance; these benefits are consistent with off-grid, sustainable, and regenerative living tenets.

An off-grid farmhouse's long-term sustainability and feasibility mainly depend on its capacity to produce renewable energy. Making educated judgments about putting renewable energy systems into place involves evaluating the availability of sunshine for solar energy, wind patterns for wind energy, and water supplies for micro-hydro power. An area rich in natural resources for energy production supports off-grid living's self-sufficiency objectives and lessens dependency on conventional power sources.

The social and community characteristics of the area you choose for an off-grid farm should be considered. Off-grid life frequently stresses independence and self-sufficiency, but the neighborhood may also be a helpful resource. Interacting with like-minded people, participating in community projects, and learning about the values of the area improve your off-grid experience and foster a feeling of cooperation and a common goal.

Wildlife and the surrounding natural environment enhance the whole atmosphere and experience of living off the grid. A biodiversity-rich area that offers access to scenic views and outdoor activities can improve your quality of life and supply more resources for sustainable living. A stronger bond with the land and the ideals of off-grid life may be fostered by the peace of a natural setting, which can also be a source of inspiration and well-being.

Adaptability and future-proofing are crucial when choosing a site for your off-grid homestead. Proactive planning that guarantees your homestead's long-term sustainability and resilience is made possible by anticipating changes in the climate, environmental circumstances, and socioeconomic aspects. Selecting a site with an eye toward the future might help your off-grid lifestyle remain flexible when faced with changing obstacles.

In summary, picking the ideal site for an off-grid homestead is a complex process that requires a thorough analysis of social, legal, environmental, and practical considerations. It entails striking a careful balance between the available natural resources, applicable laws, local dynamics, and your goals for a self-sufficient and sustainable life. An off-grid homestead can only flourish if its location is carefully chosen and in line with the values of resilience, harmony with the natural world, and sustainable living.

Legal Considerations for Homesteading

Starting a homestead is a journey into a way of life-based on sustainability, self-sufficiency, and a relationship with the land. However, the legal issues surrounding homesteading are as varied and complex as the actions themselves. Homesteaders have to negotiate a complicated legal environment, which includes everything from zoning laws and land purchase to building standards and water rights, to ensure their activities comply with rules without sacrificing the independence of being a homesteader.

The purchase and ownership of land is one of the leading legal requirements for homesteading. Homesteaders must extensively study and comprehend the legal ramifications of land ownership, including property borders, easements, and title documents, despite the temptation of large acres. Avoiding legal issues and building a safe foundation for the homestead include confirming land titles, inspecting the area, and speaking with local officials.

Zoning regulations are essential in defining what kinds of activities are allowed on a property. Zoning laws in many locations define specific land uses, such as residential, commercial, or agricultural. To guarantee that your residence complies with local standards, you must comprehend the zoning laws that apply to it. While there may be unique laws or exemptions for homesteading in some places, getting the required permissions and licenses is essential to avoiding legal issues.

Legal concerns about water rights are crucial, particularly in areas with a water shortage or conflicting interests. To correctly manage water resources, it is essential to comprehend the rules controlling water use, such as previous appropriation schemes and riparian rights. Securing the required licenses for rainwater gathering, wells, and other water sources guarantees household sustainability and legal compliance.

A primary legal consideration for homesteaders looking to build or alter structures on their land is navigating building codes. Building regulations are set to guarantee the security and sound construction of homes, and adherence to them is frequently required. Homesteaders who want to ensure that their constructions follow safety regulations and align with sustainable and self-sufficient living must become knowledgeable about local building rules, secure the necessary permits, and collaborate with skilled specialists.

One of the main components of homesteading is off-grid living, which brings with it special legal issues about waste management and alternative energy sources. Installing renewable energy equipment, such as wind turbines or solar panels, necessitates following local laws and obtaining permits. Comparably, to ensure acceptable and lawful off-grid living, putting into practice sustainable waste management techniques like greywater systems or composting toilets requires adherence to environmental standards.

Regarding farming, animal husbandry, and food production, homesteaders who engage in agricultural activities must consider farming rules and regulations. Complying with pesticide restrictions, following animal management requirements, and understanding the organic certification procedures are essential for ethical farming practices and compliance. Furthermore, investigating neighborhood farmer's markets, community-supported agriculture (CSA) projects, or farm-to-table efforts might lead to opportunities for the lawful and advantageous distribution of products made on homesteads.

Even though they are sometimes disregarded, easements have legal implications that might affect homesteaders, particularly if their property is impacted by utility or access easements. Homesteaders should carefully review property records to find any easements in place and comprehend how they may affect how their land is used. Legal advice can provide light on easement rights and limitations, allowing the homestead to maintain its intended autonomy while adhering to legal requirements.

For homesteaders who want to leave a legacy and pass down their property to future generations, estate planning is an essential legal consideration. A thorough estate plan that incorporates trusts, wills, and succession planning guarantees that the homestead's future will align with the homesteader's goals. Attorneys focusing on estate planning can advise reducing tax consequences and enabling an easy asset transfer.

Understanding the effects of local and state laws on schooling is another necessary skill for navigating the legal aspects of homesteading. To guarantee the legal recognition of their educational attempts, homesteaders who choose homeschooling or other alternative education methods must adhere to applicable legislation. While maintaining the homesteader's dedication to comprehensive and self-directed learning, researching and following local education authorities' standards for homeschooling can help build a positive relationship with them.

For homesteaders that place a high priority on ecological care, environmental restrictions, and conservation laws are crucial legal issues. Specific laws designed to safeguard natural resources may apply to certain activities like reforestation, land conservation, and animal habitat protection. To ensure their actions comply with the law and support more significant conservation initiatives, homesteaders might interact with land trusts, environmental organizations, and local conservation programs.

Legal considerations of community engagement go beyond just regulatory compliance. Building strong bonds with nearby residents, law enforcement, and neighborhood associations may help develop a network of support that recognizes and values homesteaders' objectives. A cooperative atmosphere that improves the homestead's legal position in the community may be created by open communication, involvement in neighborhood projects, and a proactive attitude to resolving issues.

In homesteading, maintaining legal compliance necessitates constant attention to detail and flexibility. A homesteader's relationship with the legal system can be amicable if they keep up with regulatory changes, obtain legal advice when needed, and communicate openly with the appropriate authorities. By promoting favorable laws for homesteading and spreading awareness of the advantages of a sustainable and independent life, homesteaders may actively influence local policy.

In summary, managing the legal ramifications of homesteading necessitates a comprehensive strategy that considers construction rules, water rights, zoning laws, land ownership, and several other regulatory factors. Homesteaders must maintain compliance with local authorities, the legal community, and the sustainability and self-sufficiency principles while interacting with them. Homesteaders may farm their land, raise their children, and participate in the larger community within a legal framework that supports their vision of deliberate and harmonious living when they fully understand the legal environment.

Essential Infrastructure for Off-Grid Living

Setting out to live off the grid requires a solid dedication to sustainability, self-sufficiency, and coexisting peacefully with the environment. Homesteaders need to carefully develop and construct necessary infrastructure that serves their basic requirements and adheres to environmental responsibility standards to prosper in this alternative lifestyle. An off-grid existence that is effective and satisfying requires the development of off-grid solid infrastructure, which includes everything from waste management and communication to energy generation and water delivery.

Off-grid life is fundamentally based on energy independence; thus, finding a dependable and sustainable energy source is crucial. One prominent and environmentally beneficial option for off-grid homesteads is solar electricity. A reliable and sustainable power source is produced by solar panels that are appropriately positioned to catch sunlight and convert it into electricity. Wind turbines may also capture wind energy; micro-hydro devices can create power using water flow. Integrating several renewable energy sources guarantees an off-grid, robust energy infrastructure that continues to operate across various weather circumstances.

Any farm must have access to water as it is essential to life, and off-grid living necessitates careful planning for water supply. For their water needs, off-grid homesteaders frequently rely on wells, rainwater collection systems, or adjacent bodies of water. Rainwater harvesting systems that are well-maintained and well-designed may collect and store rainwater for use by livestock, irrigation, and drinking. Putting into practice water-saving techniques, such as low-flow plumbing, and adequate irrigation, enhances the off-grid philosophy of prudent resource management.

Off-grid living places an even greater emphasis on waste management, making careful efforts to reduce trash and recycle essential. Composting toilets are a sustainable substitute for conventional sewage systems, as they turn human waste into nutrient-rich compost that may be used as plant fertilizer. Greywater systems reduce water waste and encourage a closed-loop water cycle by diverting and filtering water from sinks and showers for non-potable purposes. Adherents of zero-waste homesteading develop inventive ways to recycle and repurpose items, integrating their way of life with the regenerative concepts of off-grid living.

Communication infrastructure is an often overlooked but essential part of off-grid life, particularly for people trying to balance connectedness and seclusion. For informational and emergency purposes, as well as for community involvement, off-grid homesteaders can keep linked to the outside world by setting up dependable communication channels like satellite internet or two-way radio systems. The overall quality of off-grid life is improved when the necessity for communication is balanced with the need for isolation.

For off-grid houses to remain comfortable and sustainable—especially in areas with harsh weather— heating and cooling solutions are essential. Heat may be produced effectively and sustainably with wood-burning stoves that run on wood that has been obtained responsibly. With the help of components like thermal mass and strategic orientation, passive solar architecture maximizes the use of natural sunshine for heating during the winter. It keeps the interior cool during the summer. Carefully considered insulation and energy-efficient building materials help create an off-grid, climate-responsive infrastructure with the least negative environmental effect possible.

Food production is essential to off-grid homesteaders' aspirations for self-sufficiency, and building a productive and long-lasting agricultural infrastructure is crucial. Using favorable environments, animals, and crops, varied and resilient food systems are produced according to permaculture principles. Greenhouses or cold frames make An extended growing season possible, allowing for year-round farming. Hydroponics and aquaponics provide creative answers for productive and space-saving food production. Off-grid homesteaders who prioritize regenerative farming methods not only meet their food needs but also improve the ecological health of their land.

An off-grid homestead's storage facilities are its foundation, offering safe, well-organized places for tools, crops, and other necessities. Root cellars are intended to keep perishables like fruits and vegetables fresher for longer by keeping a constant, low temperature. Tools and equipment are kept in orderly sheds or barns, which helps homesteaders manage their land and resources effectively. The off-grid infrastructure is more resilient to distant life's hardships when equipped with sturdy and weatherproof storage options.

Off-grid lifestyle transportation concerns include realistic and sustainable ways to go around the property and reach neighboring resources. Off-road vehicles fueled by electricity or biofuel complement off-grid living's environmental awareness. Using alternate forms of mobility, such as bicycles or carts propelled by animals, also encourages a low-impact and energy-saving method of traveling around the property. Carefully designing paths and access points improves the off-grid infrastructure's overall usability and accessibility.

Off-grid homesteads must take security precautions since their isolated settings may provide particular difficulties. The homestead's safety and protection are improved by installing security infrastructure, such as strategically positioned obstacles, motion-activated lights, and video cameras. Furthermore, community cooperation and communication are essential for building a watchful and supportive network that gives off-grid homesteaders a sense of security.

In summary, developing the necessary infrastructure for off-grid life necessitates a deliberate, comprehensive strategy that aligns with the values of environmental responsibility, sustainability, and self-sufficiency. To build a solid off-grid infrastructure, homesteaders must incorporate renewable energy sources, prudent water management, waste minimization techniques, and resilient agricultural systems. Off-grid homesteaders may develop a lifestyle that satisfies their requirements and adds to the larger philosophy of sustainable and harmonious living with the land by adopting a thoughtful and regenerative approach to every aspect of their infrastructure.

CHAPTER III

Sustainable Energy Solutions

Solar Power Systems

Solar power is a game-changer in the search for sustainable energy solutions since it harnesses the sun's abundant and renewable energy to create electricity. Photovoltaic (PV) panels, inverters, and related parts comprise solar power systems, which have developed into a more flexible and widely available way to generate sustainable energy. This section examines the essential elements, operating theories, applications, environmental effects, and prospects of solar power systems to illuminate how they can change the face of energy worldwide.

Photovoltaic panels, sometimes called solar panels, are the main energy-harvesting element in the center of every solar power system. These panels are made of semiconductor materials, usually silicon-based, that go through photovoltaics when exposed to sunlight. When sunlight's photons hit a semiconductor material, they liberate electrons and produce an electric current. The configuration of solar cells determines the overall capacity of the solar power system within a panel and the interconnection of numerous panels. Thanks to materials science and manufacturing developments, solar panels are now a practical and affordable alternative for various applications. They have also become more efficient.

An essential function of inverters is to change the direct current (DC) produced by solar panels into alternating current (AC) that may be used in buildings, commercial spaces, and the electrical grid. Inverters allow solar power to seamlessly integrate into current electrical systems, while solar panels provide DC electricity. Advanced features like Maximum Power Point Tracking (MPPT), which adjusts to changing solar conditions to maximize energy conversion efficiency, are frequently found in modern inverters. Furthermore, the dependability of solar power systems is increased by microinverters, which are affixed to individual solar panels and provide improved performance monitoring and fault detection capabilities.

One of the main factors influencing the broader acceptance of solar power systems is their environmental influence. Solar energy produces electricity without releasing greenhouse gases, in contrast to traditional fossil fuel-based energy sources, which helps lower carbon footprints and slow climate change. Compared to the environmental expenses associated with non-renewable energy sources, the life cycle analysis of solar panels shows that the manufacture, installation, and disposal of these panels have a substantially smaller environmental effect. The long-term sustainability of solar power systems gets even more appealing as technology advances and solar panel recycling schemes proliferate.

Solar power systems are used in various industries, demonstrating their adaptability and versatility. A decentralized and sustainable energy source is offered in residential settings via solar panels incorporated into building materials or placed on rooftops. In addition to lessening their reliance on the grid for power, homeowners may also profit from net metering schemes, which allow them to feed back surplus energy they create into the system in exchange for payment. Solar power systems help satisfy the energy needs of significant buildings in the commercial and industrial sectors. They also provide possible cost savings and correspond with corporate sustainability goals.

Solar power systems are a lifesaver in remote and off-grid locations, offering electrical access when conventional power infrastructure is nonexistent or unstable. Communities may now satisfy their basic energy demands for communication, lighting, and powering necessary appliances using solar-powered gadgets and portable solar panels. Using solar power to democratize energy access might help close the energy gap and empower neglected areas.

Another creative use is the use of solar energy in agriculture. Solar-powered pumps provide an environmentally friendly alternative to electric or diesel irrigation systems. This lowers farmers' operating expenses while supporting environmental sustainability and energy independence in the agriculture industry.

Solar power systems also contribute to the rise of electric cars (EVs). Solar charging stations help make mobility more environmentally friendly by using solar energy to recharge EV batteries. This use of solar energy in the vehicle industry aligns with more significant initiatives to cut carbon emissions and switch to greener, cleaner mobility alternatives.

Prospects for solar power systems are bright, thanks to continuous technological breakthroughs and growing public awareness of the need for sustainable energy sources. Emerging technologies like solar tracking systems and thin-film solar cells aim to increase the affordability and efficiency of solar power generation. Batteries and other energy storage devices are increasingly being used as standard parts of solar power systems, allowing for the storage of extra energy for use in times of low light or power outages.

Large-scale solar panel installations in open spaces, or "solar farms," are becoming increasingly popular to produce substantial amounts of renewable energy. By directly feeding electricity into the grid, these solar farms can aid in the broader shift to a more sustainable and clean energy mix. Furthermore, developments in building-integrated photovoltaics (BIPV) enable solar panels to be subtly incorporated into building designs, improving the buildings' visual appeal while using solar energy.

To sum up, solar power systems fundamentally change how we produce and use energy. With the help of inverters, solar panels, and related technologies, solar power has become a more feasible and essential part of the world's energy supply. Solar power systems have many uses, are environmentally friendly, and have a bright future. These factors make them essential for tackling the effects of climate change and advancing a more robust and sustainable energy system. Solar power systems illuminate the way to a cleaner, greener, and more sustainable future as people embrace the sun's plentiful energy.

Wind Turbines

Wind turbines are recognizable symbols of utilizing the kinetic energy of nature to produce power, and they stand tall in the search for sustainable energy sources. These imposing buildings, which frequently adorn the landscape with blades whirling in the wind, perfectly capture the shift to clean and renewable energy sources. This section explores the complex operation of wind turbines, their effects on the environment, their uses, and their continuous development to provide insight into their significance in changing the world's energy landscape.

A wind turbine's rotor, which comprises many aerodynamically shaped blades positioned on a central hub, is its heart. The main job of the rotor is to transform the wind's kinetic energy into mechanical energy. The wind gives a force that turns the blades when it interacts with the rotating blades. After that, a shaft attached to the hub transfers the kinetic energy to the generator. The mechanical energy in the generator is converted to electrical energy, which is then ready to be used in power networks for various purposes.

To maximize energy extraction, wind turbine blade design and engineering are essential. Usually, lightweight yet strong materials like carbon fiber composites or fiberglass are used to make blades. Carefully considered calculations are made for their design, length, and pitch to optimize performance under various wind scenarios.

Variable pitch systems and aerodynamic improvements are examples of blade design advancements that have improved the overall efficiency of contemporary wind turbines.

Wind turbines significantly impact the environment and play a crucial role in reducing the effects of climate change. Unlike conventional fossil fuel-based power plants, wind turbines produce energy without releasing greenhouse gases or other air pollutants. Compared to non-renewable energy sources, the life cycle analysis of wind turbines, which considers the manufacture, transportation, installation, and decommissioning phases, shows a favourable environmental profile. The industry's ongoing efforts to enhance manufacturing procedures and recycle turbine components could further increase the overall sustainability of wind energy.

Wind turbines are used in many industries, adding to the expanding range of renewable energy options. Located on land, onshore wind farms are familiar, particularly in ideal wind conditions. The grid receives the electricity these wind farms produce, which powers nearby towns and businesses. Built-in waterways and offshore wind farms harness the power of reliable, strong offshore winds to provide a robust renewable energy source.

Distributed wind energy systems go beyond conventional wind farms to meet the needs of localized power generation. Installing small-scale wind turbines on rooftops or public areas can serve as a decentralized energy source for residential and commercial use. These systems give users freedom and autonomy, enabling them to live entirely off the grid or only augment their energy demands. Combined with solar panels or other technologies, wind turbines added to hybrid renewable energy systems improve power generation's consistency and dependability.

Wind turbines have two uses in the field of agriculture. Farmers frequently use small-scale turbines to operate irrigation systems or produce energy for use on the farm. More giant wind turbines in rural regions encourage community-based wind projects, giving landowners another source of income and boosting local economies. Using wind energy to diversify revenue streams is consistent with sustainable farming methods.

Continuous improvements in wind turbine technology are pushing efficiency gains and opening up new avenues for using wind energy. Taller turbines with longer blades are being developed to take advantage of higher-altitude winds, which often have more constant wind speeds. Improved control systems, such as those that use artificial intelligence and predictive analytics, maximize the efficiency of turbines by modifying operations in response to current meteorological information. The cost of wind energy is decreasing thanks to innovations in manufacturing processes and materials, making it increasingly competitive with traditional energy sources.

In offshore wind energy, floating wind turbines represent a new frontier since they may be deployed in deeper oceans than conventional fixed-bottom constructions. These floating platforms increase the potential for offshore wind energy generation, which gives access to undeveloped wind resources in offshore regions. When energy storage devices like batteries are integrated with wind farms, extra electricity may be efficiently stored in high demand or low wind.

Wind turbines have many benefits, but they also have drawbacks. To appropriately address these challenges, continuous study, and community participation have been motivated by concerns about the effects of land use, wildlife interactions, and visual and acoustic consequences. Technological advancements like avian-friendly setups and quieter turbine designs alleviate these worries without sacrificing the advantages of wind energy for the environment.

In conclusion, wind turbines serve as a clean, sustainable energy source and represent the peaceful coexistence of human ingenuity and the forces of nature. A vital part of the global shift towards a sustainable energy future, wind turbines provide electricity for industry, companies, and residences through their rhythmic blade rotation. In the larger framework of renewable energy solutions, wind energy plays a crucial role due to its numerous uses, environmental advantages, and continuous technical improvements. The ever-spinning blades of wind turbines serve as beacons of hope, indicating a future where clean, abundant energy is harvested from the air we breathe as people worldwide continue to search for alternatives to conventional energy sources.

Micro-Hydro Power

Micro-hydropower is a renewable energy source that exemplifies the inventiveness of utilizing the natural flow of water to create electricity. It is noteworthy for its contribution to the field of renewable energy. Using the kinetic energy of moving water, this hydropower technology, on a smaller scale, generates both efficient and environmentally friendly energy, making it suitable for a wide range of applications. This section investigates the complexities of micro-hydro power, including its working principles, influence on the environment, its various uses, and its position in the larger landscape of renewable energy.

Simply put, micro-hydropower is a method of generating electricity by utilizing the inherent energy of flowing water to turn a turbine linked to a generator. This process transforms mechanical energy into electrical energy. Several elements, including the flow rate of water, the height of the water drop (head), and the efficiency of the turbine and generator system, all play a role in determining the quantity of energy generated. In contrast to large-scale hydroelectric dams, micro-hydro power projects are distinguished by their smaller scale and decentralized nature.

As a result, they are ideal for a broad variety of situations, ranging from off-grid towns to distant rural locations.

One of the characteristics that distinguishes micro-hydropower from other forms of hydropower is its flexibility to various water sources and terrains. Run-of-river and impoundment systems are the two primary variants of micro-hydro systems that may be distinguished from one another. Run-of-river systems create energy by redirecting a part of the water flowing from a river or stream. This is done without drastically affecting the natural flow of the water. Impoundment systems, on the other hand, need the building of a dam or weir to generate a reservoir. This produces a reservoir that enables the regulated release of water, which drives the turbine. The selection of one of these systems over another is contingent upon the particular features of the location and the amount of control needed over the flow of water.

In general, the influence that micro-hydro power has on the environment is more beneficial than the impact that conventional energy sources provide. It generates energy with low emissions of greenhouse gases. It does not rely on the burning of fuel, which contributes to a reduction in both air pollution and carbon footprints when compared to other methods. In addition, compared to more considerable hydropower developments, micro-hydro projects often impact the environment and society less. To maintain a healthy equilibrium between energy generation and the preservation of the environment, responsible site selection and project design assist in reducing the disturbance caused to local ecosystems and populations.

Micro-hydropower use may be found in a wide range of contexts, including the electrification of rural areas and the provision of power to communities that are not connected to the electric grid. In areas where there is limited access to grid energy, micro-hydro projects serve as a solution that is both dependable and sustainable. These projects provide a steady supply of power that may be used for lighting, communication, and industrial operations on a smaller scale. By supporting economic growth and contributing to the improvement of the quality of life in regions that would otherwise be neglected by traditional electricity infrastructure, these initiatives are becoming increasingly important.

There is a growing interest in micro-hydropower in the context of decentralized energy systems, which goes beyond the electrification of rural areas. Hydropower projects of a smaller size can be included in hybrid systems with other renewable energy sources, such as solar panels, wind turbines, or energy storage options. Utilizing this hybrid strategy improves the dependability and consistency of power generation by correcting for variations in the water flow or the amount of sunshine. The combination of various renewable energy sources results in the creation of robust energy systems that can satisfactorily satisfy the varied energy requirements of both communities and enterprises.

Micro-hydropower is particularly well-suited for use in agricultural applications since it provides a renewable energy source that can be utilized for irrigation and manufacturing agricultural products. Micro-hydro systems can be used by farmers working on a smaller scale to provide electricity to water pumps, hence facilitating irrigation methods and enhancing agrarian yields. In addition, mills and processing facilities driven by micro hydroelectricity make it possible to add value to agricultural goods, giving rise to prospects for the creation of money and the growth of the local economy.

Micro-hydropower is adaptable to a wide range of situations due to its scalability, allowing it to be utilized in the context of individual houses and community-based initiatives. Micro-hydro systems on a household scale can supply power for basic requirements in dwellings not connected to the grid. This provides an alternative to conventional energy sources, such as diesel generators, which are frequently hazardous to the environment. There is the potential for community-based projects to serve many families and small enterprises, therefore increasing energy independence and resilience. These projects have a bigger capacity.

Continuous developments in micro-hydro technology continue to improve its effectiveness, cost, and applicability in various application areas. There has been an increase in the amount of energy captured and a decrease in the amount of maintenance required due to improvements in turbine design, materials, and manufacturing methods. Innovations improve the total performance of micro-hydro projects in control systems and automation, which optimize power output based on the different water conditions.

In the process of decentralizing energy transformation, the importance of micro-hydropower goes beyond the simple act of electrification. Communities are given the ability to take control of local energy resources and lessen their reliance on centralized power networks, which is a significant contribution to the empowerment of communities. Local communities are frequently involved in the conception, execution, and maintenance of micro-hydro projects. This helps to cultivate a feeling of ownership and self-reliance among the populations affected.

When it comes to the varied landscape of renewable energy, micro-hydropower stands out as a solution that is both adaptable and sustainable. Its capacity to capture the flow of water for the generation of power, in conjunction with its environmental benefits and flexibility, makes it a vital participant in the worldwide endeavor to move towards energy systems that are clean and robust. Micro-hydro power projects are a prime example of the potential for small-scale innovations to greatly influence energy access, economic growth, and environmental conservation. This is particularly relevant because the world still seeks decentralized and sustainable alternatives to traditional energy sources.

CHAPTER IV

Water Management and Conservation

Collecting and Harvesting Rainwater

Investigating sustainable and alternate water sources is critical as the world's worry over water shortage grows. A workable approach that makes use of the plentiful and sometimes wasted resource that descends from the sky is rainwater collection. This section explores the fundamentals, advantages, uses, and concerns of collecting and harvesting rainwater to alleviate water shortages, encourage self-sufficiency, and support environmental sustainability.

Rainwater harvesting is collecting, holding, and using rainwater for different uses. A catchment surface, a conveyance system, storage tanks, and a distribution system are the main parts of a rainwater collecting system. Rainwater is collected on the catchment surface, which is usually the roof of a structure. The conveyance system directs water from the catchment surface to storage tanks, where it is held for later use. After rainwater is collected, the distribution system distributes it to homes and landscape irrigation locations.

Reducing reliance on traditional water sources is one of the main benefits of rainwater gathering. Through rainwater collection, people and communities may augment their water requirements without exclusively depending on groundwater or municipal water sources, particularly in areas with seasonal or intermittent rainfall. Increased resistance to droughts, centralized water distribution system breakdowns, and water shortages result from this decentralized approach to water delivery.

Rainwater harvesting systems may be installed at different sizes, ranging from substantial commercial and industrial facilities to individual homes. Rainwater from the roof can be collected at the home level by directing it through gutters and storage tanks. Water from these tanks may be used for non-potable tasks like washing cars, gardening, and toilet flushing. To satisfy specific quality requirements for applications like cooling systems or manufacturing processes, larger-scale rainwater harvesting systems in commercial and industrial contexts may include sophisticated filtering and treatment procedures.

Rainwater collection has many positive effects on the environment. The technology lessens the chance of localized floods and aids in the prevention of soil erosion by collecting rainfall before it hits the ground. Additionally, it reduces the amount of precipitation that runs off impervious surfaces and into water bodies, where contaminants might end up. Rainwater collection also eases the burden on underground aquifers, rivers, and lakes by lowering the demand for conventional water sources. Ecosystems that rely on these water sources could thus be less stressed, improving the general health of the environment.

Rainwater collection benefits the economy and the environment, especially in areas where water is expensive or scarce. Installing rainwater collecting systems can lower water costs for commercial and residential buildings and farming activities. Rainwater collection offers a valuable substitute for irrigation in agriculture, perhaps reducing dependency on costly and energy-intensive pumping from surface water or groundwater sources. Rainwater harvesting may ease the strain on stormwater management systems in metropolitan areas, negating the need to make expensive infrastructure improvements to handle surplus runoff during periods of high rainfall.

Rainwater harvesting has a wide range of uses, including both potable and non-potable ones. Rainwater does not need to be treated as drinking water for non-potable purposes like industrial operations, toilet flushing, and landscape irrigation. Rainwater may be immediately gathered and stored, and to make sure it satisfies the requirements for its intended uses, it can be subjected to straightforward filtering and disinfection procedures. Because of its adaptability, rainwater collection is especially beneficial in areas with sparse or nonexistent water treatment infrastructure.

Rainwater harvesting systems may include more advanced treatment procedures to guarantee the water satisfies drinking water regulations for potable usage. It may be necessary to use filtration, disinfection, and, in some situations, purifying techniques like distillation or reverse osmosis. Although using gathered rainwater for drinkable purposes is more prevalent in areas with developed regulatory structures and cutting-edge treatment technology, it is nevertheless a feasible solution for enhancing municipal water supply or offering a decentralized water source to underserved groups.

Nevertheless, several variables, such as climate, catchment area, storage capacity, and water demand patterns, must be met for rainwater collecting to be successful. Rainwater harvesting could not be as successful as other water supply methods as the primary water source in dry or semi-arid areas with erratic rainfall patterns. The amount and quality of gathered rainwater are contingent upon the design of the storage tanks and catchment area and routine system maintenance.

Rainwater collecting techniques are being widely used, and education and awareness are one of the main factors in this trend. The advantages of rainwater collecting may be explained to people and communities through public outreach programs, community workshops, and government efforts. These resources can also offer system design, installation, and maintenance advice. The sustainable use of rainwater in residential and commercial constructions is further promoted by encouraging the inclusion of rainwater harvesting into building standards and urban planning rules.

To sum up, rainwater collecting presents a workable and sustainable way to deal with the water shortage issues in a changing global environment. Through precipitation, people, groups, and businesses may lessen their reliance on non-renewable water sources, support environmental preservation efforts, and strengthen their ability to withstand water shortages. Gathering and storing rainwater is an essential step toward a more sustainable and water-secure future, especially as the world struggles with the effects of climate change and the increasing water demand.

Efficient Water Storage Solutions

Water, sometimes called the "elixir of life," is a limited resource that must be managed carefully, especially in light of the worldwide water shortage. Effective water storage systems are essential to maximizing the use and preservation of this valuable resource. This section explores the ideas, developments, and wide range of uses for adequate water storage. It highlights its significance for assisting communities, maintaining agriculture, and resolving issues brought on by erratic water availability.

The foundation of adequate water storage is the understanding that water is essential to human existence and industrial activities, agricultural production, and ecosystem health. Various techniques and technologies are used in efficient water storage systems to collect, hold, and distribute water in a way that reduces waste and optimizes utility.

Integrating decentralized and natural solutions is one of the core ideas behind adequate water storage. By using the local ecosystems and the natural terrain to collect and store water, these solutions lessen the need for energy-intensive procedures and centralized infrastructure. For instance, rainwater harvesting is the process of physically gathering rain off roofs or other surfaces and preserving it for use at a later time. In addition to saving water, this decentralized strategy helps replenish groundwater and lessen the effects of stormwater runoff.

Using effective water storage techniques is essential for resilient and sustainable agriculture farming because water is a crop's lifeline. Conventional techniques used for generations, including check dams and agricultural ponds, are still helpful today. During dry spells, these structures collect rainwater and runoff to supply a dependable and local water source for irrigation. Additionally, farmers can optimize water consumption by administering the appropriate quantity of water in the proper time to maximize crop yields while avoiding waste thanks to advances like intelligent irrigation systems and soil moisture monitoring.

New and advanced water storage technologies that meet a variety of purposes and circumstances have been made possible by technological innovation. Large amounts of water may be stored underground in an ecologically responsible and space-efficient manner thanks to artificial recharge techniques and aquifers. For example, aquifer storage and recovery (ASR) systems replenish surface water in abundance by pumping excess water underground into aquifers so that it may be drawn up in times of shortage.

Water storage technologies include home and industrial uses in addition to agricultural ones. With the addition of filter and treatment units, residential rainwater collecting systems enable homeowners to consume less municipal water for non-potable purposes. Large-scale industrial water storage facilities can save water and ease the burden on nearby water sources while ensuring a consistent supply for manufacturing operations.

Adequate water storage also addresses the issues brought about by seasonal fluctuations and erratic water supplies. Storage options like dams and reservoirs act as buffers, holding onto extra water during times of abundance and releasing it at high demand. These buildings are essential to water management because they give a steady water flow for agriculture, drinking, hydropower production, and ecosystem upkeep.

While adequate water storage has many advantages,

large-scale projects must consider the environment and society. Dams, in particular, can potentially have significant ecological effects that change aquatic biodiversity and river ecosystems. Responsibly planning a water storage facility requires careful site selection, thorough environmental impact evaluations, and community participation.

Water conservation and demand management are closely

related to effective water storage technologies. The requirement for extensive water storage facilities may be reduced by optimizing water consumption using technology like drip irrigation, soil moisture monitors, and leak detection systems. Combining storage options with demand-side strategies produces a comprehensive strategy for sustainable water management.

Adequate water storage becomes critical as the

population grows and water demand rises in urban areas. Innovative water storage systems allow communities to improve water distribution, quickly identify leaks, and adapt to shifting patterns of water demand when combined with real-time monitoring and control mechanisms. In densely populated areas, this kind of intelligent infrastructure improves the overall efficiency of water usage and strengthens the resilience of urban water supply networks.

The need for adequate water storage systems grows as

the globe grapples with the twin problems of population expansion and climate change. Drastic changes in precipitation patterns, a rise in the frequency of droughts, and rising temperatures highlight the need for creative and flexible methods of storing water. Restoring wetlands and forests is one example of a nature-based approach that improves watershed health, increases water storage capacity, and fosters ecosystem resilience.

In summary, effective water storage options are essential to sustainable water management because they maintain ecosystem health and human lives by balancing water supply and demand. The range of options available, from traditional methods like rainwater harvesting to state-of-the-art innovations like subterranean aquifer storage, highlights the flexibility and agility needed to handle the intricate and ever-changing problems associated with water shortage. Adopting these solutions signifies a commitment to responsible stewardship of one of our most valuable resources and securing water for present and future generations.

Sustainable Irrigation Practices

Sustainable irrigation techniques are a shining example of responsible resource management in agriculture, where the intricate relationship between water availability and demand determines the destiny of crops and lives. This section explores how farmers, scientists, and policymakers work together to navigate the complex terrain of water use to ensure food security, preserve ecosystems, and lessen the environmental effects of traditional irrigation methods. It does this by delving into sustainable irrigation's fundamentals, innovations, and profound implications.

Sustainable irrigation fundamentally differs from traditional methods, frequently putting short-term profits ahead of long-term agricultural and environmental sustainability. Flooding fields randomly is the hallmark of conventional flood irrigation, which has long been a common technique. But this approach is infamous for being ineffective, wasting water via evaporation, runoff, and deep percolation. Conversely, sustainable irrigation techniques emphasize accuracy, effectiveness, and a comprehensive comprehension of the interplay between water, soil, and plants.

The use of precision agriculture techniques characterizes precision farming. These systems accurately adjust irrigation to the unique requirements of crops by utilizing data, sensors, and advanced analytics. Precision agriculture is best demonstrated by drip irrigation and sprinkler systems, which provide water directly to plant roots while reducing evaporation losses and guaranteeing ideal moisture levels for growth. These technologies help increase agricultural yields, which is essential in the fight for global food security and conserving water.

Sustainable irrigation techniques stress the significance of time and frequency of water supply in addition to accuracy. Weather predictions, soil moisture sensors, and sophisticated irrigation scheduling systems allow farmers to match irrigation events to the actual water needs of crops. Farmers may save water and energy expenses, lessen the chance of waterlogging and soil salinity, and limit water consumption by avoiding overwatering and managing irrigation schedules depending on current circumstances.

Agroecological methods, beyond technology fixes, are essential to sustainable irrigation techniques. Agroecology recognizes the interdependence of biodiversity, soil health, and water management and incorporates ecological ideas into agricultural systems. Agroecological techniques that improve soil water retention, lessen erosion, and foster a symbiotic relationship between crops and the environment include conservation tillage, agroforestry, and cover crops. These methods support agricultural ecosystems' resilience, general health, and sustainable water usage.

A sustainable irrigation method based on the age-old knowledge of absorbing and using precipitation is rainwater collection. This technique supports the concepts of decentralized water management and water conservation. Farmers can gather and store rainwater for use later in the dry season when there is an abundance of rain. For small-scale and subsistence farmers, rainwater collection systems combined with drip or spray irrigation provide a reliable and affordable option, especially in areas with seasonal rainfall patterns.

The idea of integrated water management is one more way that agroecological concepts and technical advancements are combined. This method acknowledges the interconnectedness of surface water and groundwater resources while considering agricultural water requirements within the larger framework of the watershed. Farmers and water managers may protect both farm production and the ecological integrity of water bodies by balancing conflicting water demands via integrated water management practices.

Effective irrigation techniques must also deal with the problems caused by brackish and salinized water, which can deplete soil fertility and impede crop development. There are techniques to lessen the effects of salinity, such as using crops that can withstand salt and targeted leaching. Through careful water application, surplus salts are flushed from the root zone and prevented from building up through precision leaching. Concurrently, farmers may utilize saline water supplies for irrigation without sacrificing yields by cultivating salt-tolerant halophyte crops.

The transition to sustainable irrigation techniques is a proactive approach to mitigating the environmental externalities linked to conventional irrigation and a reaction to resource limitations. Overdrawing water from aquifers and rivers can cause habitat loss, ecological deterioration, and declining aquatic biodiversity. Recognizing the intrinsic significance of water for environmental services, including sustaining riparian habitats, wetlands, and the health of marine ecosystems, sustainable irrigation aims to balance human agricultural operations with natural ecosystems.

Sustainable irrigation has several advantages, but institutional frameworks, socioeconomic considerations, and information distribution hinder its widespread implementation. Smallholder farmers, who comprise a sizable share of the world's agricultural sector, frequently need help restricting access to resources like money, knowledge, and technology. Through their provision of financial support, technical assistance, and capacity-building programs customized to meet the requirements of varied agricultural communities, governments, non-governmental organizations, and international organizations play a crucial role in easing the transition to sustainable irrigation.

Education and awareness efforts are among the most critical aspects of the sustainable irrigation paradigm. Farmers must have access to knowledge on the advantages of environmentally friendly methods, the availability of cutting-edge technologies, and the possible financial rewards. Providing channels for information sharing, extension services, farmer field schools, and cooperative research projects enables farmers to make well-informed choices about sustainable irrigation techniques.

In sum, adopting sustainable irrigation techniques marks a paradigm change in how we see water use in agriculture. Sustainability in irrigation goes beyond simple conservation and involves a comprehensive comprehension of the complex interrelationships among crops, soil, and water. The path to sustainable irrigation involves many different aspects, such as the integration of water management at the watershed level, agroecological concepts, and precision agricultural technology. In light of climate change, the world community must find a way to produce more food with less water. Adopting and expanding sustainable irrigation techniques is not a choice; it is essential for a resilient and food-secure future.

CHAPTER V

DIY Shelter and Living Spaces

Building Eco-Friendly Structures

Standing at a crossroads, ready to redefine its role in creating a sustainable future, the construction industry is reacting to the effects of climate change and environmental degradation that the globe is experiencing. Constructing environmentally friendly buildings has become a crucial tactic to reduce the environmental impact of human habitation, providing a peaceful cohabitation with the natural world while tackling the urgent problems of resource depletion, energy use, and waste production. This section delves into sustainable materials, energy-efficient design, and nature-inspired solutions to examine the fundamentals, advancements, and significant ramifications of building environmentally friendly structures.

The careful selection of materials that minimize environmental effects throughout their life cycle is essential to eco-friendly building. Despite their durability, traditional construction materials like steel and concrete can have significant carbon emissions, need energy-intensive production processes, and require resource extraction. Eco-friendly substitutes, such as bamboo, engineered wood, and recycled steel, impact the environment less and help preserve natural resources. Utilizing salvaged materials from demolished structures contributes to sustainability by lowering the need for new extraction and manufacturing techniques.

Sustainable building material innovations go beyond recycling and include creating new materials that use renewable resources and biodegradability. For example, plant-based bioplastics are becoming increasingly popular for use in various construction applications.

These materials are as strong and durable as conventional plastics, but because they break down organically, they have less long-term adverse environmental impact than traditional plastic trash. Similarly, mycelium's lightweight, fire-resistant, and insulating qualities—the fungal root structure—make it a promising construction material.

The foundation of environmentally friendly architecture is energy efficiency, which focuses on reducing a building's energy use through clever design and incorporating renewable energy sources. By utilizing the natural environment to control lighting and temperature, passive design principles lessen the need for mechanical heating, ventilation, and air conditioning (HVAC) systems. Critical components of passive design are efficient orientation, well-placed windows, and the utilization of thermal mass to maximize interior space without excessive energy.

Technologies for renewable energy are essential to the sustainable powering of environmentally friendly buildings; by providing clean, renewable energy alternatives to traditional energy sources, solar, wind, and geothermal technologies help lessen dependency on fossil fuels and reduce greenhouse gas emissions. By combining cutting-edge building-integrated photovoltaic systems with more efficient solar panels, buildings may produce electricity, enhancing grid resilience and lowering reliance on centralized power supply.

Living walls and green roofs are prime examples of how nature can coexist with the built environment. Urban green areas are created, stormwater runoff is decreased, insulation is provided, and green roofs are covered with vegetation. They also support biodiversity by providing homes for insects, plants, and birds. Living walls with vertical plant gardens look better and help purify the air by absorbing toxins and releasing oxygen. In addition to improving a structure's environmental efficiency, these nature-inspired design choices also improve inhabitants' well-being by encouraging a connection with the natural world.

Another essential component of environmentally friendly building is water conservation, which emphasizes the wise use of this valuable resource. Greywater recycling systems collect and clean wastewater from showers, washing machines, and sinks for irrigation and toilet flushing, among other non-potable applications. Water usage is further reduced via low-flow fixtures and rainwater harvesting, which relieves pressure on nearby water sources and wastewater treatment plants. In addition to supporting sustainable water management, these actions help the overarching objective of building resilient and adaptable urban ecosystems.

Inspired by the patterns and functions seen in nature, the idea of biomimicry has emerged as a tenet of environmentally sustainable building. The form of termite mounds influences ventilation systems, while the lotus effect inspires self-cleaning surfaces. Biomimicry provides creative solutions that improve the sustainability and efficiency of buildings. This method maximizes energy efficiency and promotes a better comprehension of the complex balance in natural ecosystems.

The principles of environmentally friendly construction apply to individual buildings and the planning and design of sustainable communities. Incorporating green areas, walkways convenient for pedestrians, and mixed land-use zoning helps build thriving, resilient, socially integrated neighborhoods. Accessibility to public transit is emphasized in sustainable urban planning, which lessens the need for private automobiles and encourages a move toward more environmentally friendly forms of mobility.

The building industry must undergo a paradigm change to realize eco-friendly structures. This transition is driven by innovative technology, a collaborative approach among stakeholders, and a dedication to environmental stewardship. Structures may be assessed and recognized for their sustainability using frameworks provided by green building certifications like BREEAM (Building Research Establishment Environmental Assessment Method) and LEED (Leadership in Energy and

Environmental Design). Through laws, subsidies, and consumer preferences, governments, trade groups, and builders all have a crucial part to play in encouraging and rewarding environmentally friendly building techniques.

To sum up, creating environmentally friendly buildings is a revolutionary step toward a built environment that is more robust and sustainable. The building sector can take the lead in tackling global environmental issues by adopting sustainable materials, energy-efficient design, and nature-inspired solutions. Beyond the obvious advantages of resource-saving and less ecological effects, eco-friendly building practices help create healthier, more livable environments that put the health of their occupants and the environment first. Building environmentally friendly structures is a ray of hope in the face of global concern about sustainable development, as it represents the prospect of balancing human demands with the fragile balance of the natural world.

Creative Tiny Homes and Cabins

A fascinating counter-narrative is being told by the increasing popularity of imaginative little homes and cabins in a society where large mansions and the unrelenting quest for luxury are commonplace. These tiny homes, distinguished by their efficient use of space and minimalist design, have drawn the interest of those looking for a different kind of living that emphasizes sustainability, simplicity, and a stronger bond with the natural world. This section delves into the inventive designs, distinctive features, and significant lifestyle changes that come with the varied terrain of artistic tiny houses and cabins.

The clever use of limited space is one of the distinguishing features of inventive compact homes. The ingenious tactics architects and designers use to create these little homes optimize usefulness without compromising comfort. Convertible couches and tables are multipurpose furniture that maximizes living spaces for various uses. Utilizing vertical dimensions, fold-down beds, secret storage rooms, and loft areas make the most of every square foot available. These creative space-saving ideas upend conventional ideas about what a home should be and demonstrate that a happy living environment can be any size.

Creative tiny homes are appealing because they promote a more sustainable lifestyle and use available space excellently. Diminished environmental effects, lower energy usage, and a decreased need for building materials are all associated with smaller physical footprints. To further reduce their environmental impact, many tiny homes have eco-friendly amenities like rainwater collecting systems, composting toilets, and solar panels. Tiny house living's inherent sustainability has drawn attention as a workable paradigm for ecologically aware habitation in a world where climate change and resource depletion concerns are becoming more pressing.

Creative tiny homes can offer compact living and serve as a platform for unique architectural design and personal expression. Architects and do-it-yourselfers have taken up the task of creating visually beautiful and valuable homes. The variety of styles, which range from chic modern designs to charming cottages with rustic charm, represents the individual interests and likes of the homes' occupants. The tiny home movement has developed into a fertile field for avant-garde architecture, demonstrating that imagination is unrestricted by small spaces.

Beyond only the exterior, small dwellings can represent a radical change in living. Making the purposeful decision to reduce and downsize is a way to put experiences and quality before numbers. People who live in tiny houses frequently talk about how liberating it is to give up stuff that isn't required and embrace a more deliberate, well-curated lifestyle. As many small house communities emphasize cooperation, mutual assistance, and a sense of belonging beyond the actual bounds of individual dwellings, this intentional living ethos also extends to a focus on community and shared resources.

The ability to live a nomadic and mobile lifestyle is one of the unique features of tiny house living. Certain small homes may be moved and explored without compromising the comforts of home since they are designed to be mobile. This freedom from the traditional confines of a permanent home aligns with the increasing demand for an adaptable and adventurous lifestyle. These transportable tiny homes provide a dynamic and constantly evolving living experience, whether parked in a woodland glade, perched on a mountainside, or tucked away by the coast.

Tiny houses are famous for reasons other than just being practical for day-to-day living; they represent a more significant cultural movement to reconsider how we relate to space, consumerism, and the environment. Tiny dwellings encourage us to reevaluate the meaning of home by challenging conventional standards that correlate success and pleasure with dwelling size. This movement is about more than just cutting down; it's about reevaluating our principles and encouraging a more deliberate and attentive way of living in the world.

It's essential to recognize that living in a compact house has specific difficulties. For people who want to adopt tiny living, there may be obstacles due to zoning laws, construction rules, and the challenges of finding an appropriate site. Furthermore, the restricted living and storage capacity may be a big adjustment for those used to larger spaces. Notwithstanding these difficulties, the rising demand for inventive tiny homes highlights a significant societal movement toward a more environmentally friendly and thoughtful style of life.

In conclusion, the appeal of uniquely designed tiny houses and cabins is their capacity to challenge preconceived ideas about what constitutes a home. These little homes are the epitome of creativity, sustainability, and a rethinking of the interaction between people and their environments. Tiny houses are part of a cultural trend promoting deliberate living, simplicity, and a healthy cohabitation with the environment beyond their unique architectural designs and creative ways to save space. Innovative tiny houses invite us to reflect on the idea that sometimes less is better and that focused, mindful living is the key to an entire existence, whether they are used as a primary dwelling, a weekend getaway, or a nomadic journey.

Off-Grid Renovation Projects

The appeal of off-grid living has spurred a surge of remodeling projects that try to create self-sufficient and sustainable houses in a world that is becoming increasingly tied to centralized electricity networks and municipal utilities. Off-grid renovation projects reflect a paradigm change in how we conceive about and interact with our living environments. These projects challenge traditional concepts of dependency on resources external to the home. This section goes into the varied world of off-grid remodeling, examining the reasons for such projects, the most important factors to consider, and the novel technology driving this disruptive approach to sustainable living.

The desire to become more self-sufficient and have a

minor environmental impact is frequently the impetus for developing off-grid remodeling projects. Especially in isolated or rural locations, where access to these services may be difficult, the old paradigm of depending on centralized utilities for energy, water, and waste management can be restricting. This is especially true in settings where these services are difficult to obtain. Renovators working on off-grid projects aim to free themselves from these limitations and adopt a more independent lifestyle in line with sustainability and resilience. Off-grid renovations are undertaken by persons with a shared goal of gaining better control over their living conditions. A dedication to environmental stewardship, a desire for energy independence, or a search for a more straightforward way of life may drive this goal.

If you want your off-grid remodeling project to be successful, integrating renewable energy sources should be done carefully. Solar power is a technology that stands out as a cornerstone since photovoltaic panels can convert sunlight into energy to provide electricity to the home. Solar panel efficiency, battery storage systems, and inverter technology have all seen considerable advancements in recent years, which have led to significant improvements in the viability and dependability of off-grid solar solutions. It is common practice for renovators to build their energy systems in a modular and scalable manner, which enables future additions or alterations to be made in response to changing energy requirements. A varied and resilient energy portfolio may be achieved by utilizing wind turbines, micro-hydro power systems, and solar electricity, all of which contribute to using the natural resources already accessible in particular regions.

Another essential component of off-grid restorations is water autonomy, which calls for developing novel approaches to procuring, storing, and treating water. Rainwater harvesting systems, in conjunction with cutting-edge filtration and purification technologies, allow renovators to collect rainwater and use it for their own household requirements. To further optimize water consumption, greywater recycling systems clean and repurpose water from sinks, showers, and washing machines for purposes that do not require potable water, such as irrigation or flushing toilets. Not only can these measures improve water self-sufficiency, but they also help to conserve local water resources, which is especially important in regions inclined to experience water scarcity.

Waste management becomes a central focus during off-grid restorations, emphasizing a closed-loop approach to reduce the negative impact on the environment. Composting toilets, for example, convert human waste into compost rich in nutrients, removing the requirement for conventional sewage systems. Recycling and composting methods are included in daily routines, which reduce the amount of trash produced and encourage a more environmentally responsible approach to consumption. During the building and remodeling, off-grid renovators frequently adopt a mindset emphasizing ingenuity, reusing resources, and limiting waste.

Off-grid renovations involve more than just the technical concerns of energy, water, and waste management; they also involve a comprehensive reevaluation of lifestyle choices and the home's architecture. One of the most critical aspects of off-grid houses is the implementation of passive design principles, which involve utilizing the natural environment to control the temperature and lighting. Thermal mass, strategic orientation, and efficient insulation help maintain acceptable interior conditions without heavily relying on mechanical heating or cooling systems. In addition, to further optimize energy use, renovators give priority to energy-efficient appliances, LED lighting, and smart home technology.

Living off the grid encourages a more profound connection to the natural world and a more purposeful engagement with the ecosystem surrounding each individual. Those interested in renovating frequently select areas with abundant natural resources, breathtaking scenery, and the opportunity for sustainable agriculture. Incorporating green roofs, edible landscaping, and outdoor living areas that celebrate the beauty of the local ecology is one way off-grid houses become a harmonic extension of the natural surroundings. Combining contemporary conveniences with the peace of the natural environment results in a one-of-a-kind combination that provides both comfort and a feeling of being away from it all.

Negotiating regulatory frameworks, ensuring legal compliance, and resolving the upfront expenditures connected with the implementation of renewable energy and water systems are all inherent challenges in off-grid restorations.

In addition, there is a learning curve for those accustomed to the amenities of urban living, which requires them to adjust to a more hands-on and conscious approach to their day-to-day lives. Homeowners who renovate their homes off the grid view these problems as opportunities for personal development, education, and a more profound connection to the world's natural cycles.

In conclusion, off-grid rehabilitation projects are characterized by a transformational approach to sustainable living. These projects exemplify the values of self-sufficiency, resilience, and environmental stewardship. These initiatives go beyond implementing environmentally friendly technology; instead, they represent a comprehensive transformation in lifestyle, changing the relationship between persons and the environments in which they live. Off-grid renovations serve as a light of innovation when the globe is grappling with the urgency of moving to more sustainable practices. These renovations demonstrate the possibility of building houses that reduce their impact on the environment and improve the well-being and autonomy of the people who live in them.

CHAPTER VI

Food Independence and Gardening

Planning and Designing a Homestead Garden

Starting a homestead frequently stems from a long-standing desire to establish harmony with nature, promote self-sufficiency, and connect with the land. The homestead garden, a dynamic and vital element that offers nourishment, beauty, and a deep connection to the cycles of growth and rebirth, is our project's center. A homestead garden's planning and design are both an art and a science, involving careful consideration of the land's characteristics, the climate, and the particular requirements and tastes of the homesteaders. This section examines the many aspects of designing a successful and aesthetically beautiful homestead garden, exploring the fundamental ideas, practical design aspects, and sustainable methods that make up this vital component of homesteading.

A detailed study of the local climate, soil, and ecological environment is essential to the planning and design of a homestead garden. Homesteaders must perform a site study that evaluates elements, including wind patterns, sunshine exposure, and vegetation. Making wise choices about plant selection, arrangement, and overall garden design is based on this understanding. Permaculture principles and other sustainable and regenerative methods stress the value of utilizing the land's natural characteristics rather than fighting against them. Homestead gardens may flourish in balance with the surrounding ecosystems by using the natural resources of their surroundings.

Choosing the right plant kinds is critical to designing a homestead garden. Aside from personal taste in food, homesteaders must also consider the crops' nutritional worth, climatic tolerance, and biodiversity-promoting potential. Crop diversification helps control pests, improves soil health, and increases the garden's resilience. By combining perennial plants with annual crops, such as fruit trees and veggies, you may create a more diversified and stable ecosystem in your garden by adding layers of complexity. A time-honored technique, companion planting is planting plants deliberately to complement one another, encourage reciprocal development, and naturally repel pests.

When planning the homestead garden's layout, economy and practicality must be balanced with aesthetic appeal. The garden may be divided into zones according to the water needed, how much sunlight it receives, and how often care has to be done. For ease of access, high-use areas like herb gardens or kitchen gardens may be located nearer to the homestead, but orchards and perennial crops are best suited for locations with lots of sunlight and space. To create a warm and visually appealing atmosphere that promotes interaction with the garden, pathways, water features, and seating places can be incorporated into the design.

Planning a homestead garden requires careful consideration of sustainable water management, especially in areas with erratic rainfall patterns. Drip irrigation, rainwater gathering systems, and effective watering schedules all maximize water use and lessen dependency on outside sources. Mulching is another crucial technique that improves soil fertility, controls temperature, inhibits weed growth and preserves moisture. Homesteaders may make garden ecosystems resilient and ecologically conscious by emphasizing water conservation and efficiency.

The foundation of any fruitful homestead garden is healthy soil. Homesteaders must test their soil to evaluate the pH, nitrogen levels, and general soil structure. Compost and well-rotted manure are examples of organic additions that provide the soil with vital nutrients and improve its capacity to hold water. Soil fertility and structure are further enhanced by cover cropping, a technique in which certain plants are planted to cover and shield the soil during inactivity. The focus on creating and preserving good soil is a reflection of homesteaders' long- term dedication to growing a garden that is both abundant and regenerative.

Homestead gardeners strive to establish self-sustaining ecosystems where waste is reduced, and resources are recycled within the garden by adhering to permaculture principles. For example, composting turns garden waste and leftover food into nutrient-rich soil additives. Adding animal systems, such as hens for manure production and pest management, gives the homestead an additional layer of ecological balance. Homestead gardens are a living example of sustainability and resilience because they create a closed-loop system in which the outputs of one element become the inputs for another.

When developing a homestead garden, the seasons and their natural cycles are crucial considerations. Crop rotation, which is shifting crops from one season to the next, enhances nutrient cycling, reduces the risk of soil-borne illnesses, and preserves the general health of the soil. Homesteaders may optimize their production all year long by planning their plantings according to the local growing season and frost dates. By planting crops at different stages of maturity, succession planting guarantees a steady supply of fresh products.

It's essential to consider homestead garden design from an aesthetic perspective. Not only is beauty in the garden decorative, but it also enhances the homestead's general satisfaction and well-being. A thoughtful mix of creative arrangements, landscaping features, and flowering plants improves the garden's aesthetic appeal and fosters reflection and a sense of connection to the natural world. Incorporating native plants tailored to the regional environment promotes biodiversity and shows care for the environment.

In summary, creating a homestead garden is a dynamic and incredibly fulfilling process combining aesthetic expression and functional considerations. Homesteaders who set out on this trip take on the role of stewards of the land, cooperating with the natural world to provide an abundant and sustainable food source. The homestead garden is more than just an assortment of plants; it is evidence of the tenacity, ingenuity, and devotion of people committed to building a more peaceful and independent way of life.

Implementing Permaculture Principles

Derived from the words "permanent agriculture" or "permanent culture," permaculture is a design concept that goes beyond simple farming or gardening and represents a sustainable way of living sustainably modeled after natural ecosystems. Fundamentally, permaculture aims to develop regenerative systems that emulate the diversity and resilience of nature, promoting settings in which people live in harmony with the planet. This section explores the application of permaculture principles, looking at the fundamental ideas that underpin this transformational design philosophy and how people might use them to build autonomous, regenerative systems.

Observing natural processes and patterns is one of the core tenets of permaculture. Permaculturists learn about the interactions between various elements, energy flows, and the cyclical patterns that control natural systems by closely studying the nuances of ecosystems. The design process is informed by this foundation of observation, which enables permaculturists to operate in harmony with the innate knowledge of the natural environment. It promotes a systematic and deliberate approach in which comprehension comes before action, and design solutions naturally flow from patterns seen.

Creating with nature, not against it, is a fundamental component of the permaculture design concept. Permaculturists aim to smoothly incorporate human settlements and systems into the natural environment rather than imposing complex buildings. This integration requires careful consideration of the site's unique features, terrain, and water flows. Methods like contour planting, in which crops are positioned by the land's natural contours, minimize soil erosion and maximize water retention. Permaculture designs foster a feeling of place and create harmonious, functional ecosystems by using the natural elements of the environment.

A fundamental tenet of permaculture is its emphasis on building resilient and diversified systems. Permaculturists create landscapes with various plants, animals, and microbes to mimic the biodiversity seen in natural ecosystems. Growing many crops in one area, or polyculture, improves system stability by lowering the possibility of pest and disease outbreaks. Companion planting is a cooperative approach to permaculture design whereby plants that complement one another are planted together. This variety creates a web of interdependencies that reflects the complexity of natural ecosystems, extending beyond the domain of plants to encompass animals, fungi, and other elements.

Designing with efficiency and ease in mind, the idea of "zones" is a practical application of permaculture concepts. Zones classify design items according to how frequently they are used and how close they are to the main living area. Kitchen gardens and herbs are examples of high-intensity, often utilized components found in Zone 1, which is closest to the house. Zone 5 represents the wild or undisturbed areas, with use intensities decreasing as one proceeds from the center. By strategically placing pieces, this zoning system maximizes energy and resource efficiency while guaranteeing that necessary components are conveniently accessible.

Within the context of permaculture design, water is a valuable resource that should be managed and conserved responsibly. Permaculture water management relies heavily on rainwater collecting, keyline design—a technique for regulating water flow on hilly terrain—and swales, contour ditches designed to capture and slow water. Permaculturists build water-efficient systems that encourage plant development, lessen dependency on outside water sources, and increase overall resilience against climatic instability by optimizing the absorption and retention of rainfall.

"Stacking functions" is a method that demonstrates the efficiency that permaculture design embodies. This idea entails choosing components that have several uses inside the system. For example, when the hens graze in the garden, a chicken coop may act as a natural pest control method and produce eggs. In addition to yielding food, fruit trees generate habitat for beneficial insects, offer shade, and enhance the soil quality. Permaculturists optimize the whole system's productivity and synergy by deliberately selecting components that serve numerous purposes.

Moreover, permaculture highly values soil health since it is considered the cornerstone of resilient and fruitful ecosystems. Composting, mulching, and cover crops are some practices that improve soil fertility, structure, and moisture retention. The "no-till" method protects the complex network of microbial life essential to the cycling of nutrients by preventing mechanical disturbance of the soil. Regenerating damaged soils into vibrant, nutrient-rich conditions that enable vigorous plant development is the goal of permaculture design.

Permaculture values are fundamentally about community and collaboration. The ideology acknowledges that sharing information, resources, and labor is crucial to building strong, resilient communities. Common areas, shared gardens, and collaborative projects that promote a sense of community and support among participants are frequently included in permaculture designs. This emphasis on community promotes biodiversity and ecological resilience by having a more prominent natural community and immediate human occupants.

Permaculture design incorporates energy efficiency and renewable energy sources as essential elements. For example, passive solar architecture makes the most of the sun's natural motions to maximize heating and cooling within buildings. Energy-efficient technology reduces consumption, and wind and solar power are utilized to satisfy energy demands. Permaculturists lessen their ecological footprint and promote a more sustainable and regenerative way of life by emphasizing renewable energy and efficient architecture.

In summary, applying permaculture concepts necessitates a dramatic change of viewpoint from considering the land as a resource to be mined to seeing it as a living, dynamic system that has to be nourished. This design concept promotes a careful and wise approach in which people take on the role of guardians of the land and collaborate with natural processes. By implementing permaculture concepts in their houses, gardens, and local communities, people join a broader movement to develop resilient systems, regenerative systems, and a peaceful coexistence of humans and the environment.

Animal Husbandry for Sustainable Food Production

Animal husbandry is a vital discipline that connects agriculture with holistic ecosystem management in the goal of sustainable and regenerative food production. Sustainable animal husbandry goes beyond the simple production of meat, milk, and other animal products. It encompasses a dedication to moral treatment, environmental stewardship, and the incorporation of animals into regenerative farming systems. The many facets of animal husbandry for sustainable food production are examined in this section, which also looks at the broader ramifications of rearing animals with an eye toward their welfare and the health of their ecosystems.

Considering animal welfare as a fundamental premise is essential to healthy animal agriculture. Allowing animals to engage in everyday activities, receiving a nutritious diet, and having suitable living quarters are all components of ethical care. Sustainable animal husbandry emphasizes the welfare of individual animals more than industrial farming methods, which emphasize efficiency and scale. Animals need plenty of room to roam around, graze, and act in natural ways for both physical and mental well-being. Since each animal's existence has intrinsic value, ethical treatment also includes humane handling, providing access to clean water, and receiving the necessary veterinary care.

Recognizing the importance of animals in soil fertility, insect management, and the general health of the ecosystem, holistic and regenerative farming systems include animals in the greater ecosystem. One of the most critical aspects of sustainable animal husbandry is rotational grazing, which entails rotating animals among several pasture sites so the flora can recuperate and rest. This supports healthier grasslands, better soil structure, enhanced carbon storage, and prevents overgrazing. Agroecological farming, which incorporates animals into crop rotation systems, produces synergies that improve the farming operation's sustainability.

The diversification of livestock species enhances sustainable food production and ecological resilience. Compared to high-yield varieties, traditional and heritage breeds, which have evolved to their particular settings, frequently show higher disease resistance and less environmental impact. Incorporating biodiversity into animal husbandry promotes genetic variation across populations, which lowers livestock's susceptibility to illnesses and ecological stresses. Additionally, varied systems with various species—like mixing ruminants and poultry—create mutually beneficial partnerships and have various animals serving different environmental tasks.

The preference for pasture-based systems over confinement operations is a fundamental component of sustainable animal husbandry practices. Animals raised in pasture-based or free-range environments can exhibit their natural behaviors, graze various forages, and live more naturally and stress-free lives. This contrasts the industrial paradigm of concentrated animal feeding operations (CAFOs), which confine animals to cramped quarters and frequently unhygienic settings. In addition to putting the welfare of the animals first, pasture-based systems also improve soil health, lessen the need for artificial inputs, and help build resilient, regenerative landscapes.

An essential part of sustainable animal husbandry is managed grazing, which entails carefully organizing and rearranging the movement of cattle among several paddocks. This strategy permits grazed regions to rest and regenerate while imitating the migratory patterns of wild herbivores. Animal grazing promotes microbiological activity, nitrogen cycling, and soil fertility through dung and trampling. Grazing systems that are appropriately managed promote the establishment of various plant species, enhance soil structure, and retain more water, all of which help create vital and productive ecosystems.

It is crucial to understand "closed-loop systems" in sustainable animal husbandry. As a result of animal digestion, manure is valued as a resource rather than as trash. Using dung as fertilizer in the farming system may minimize environmental damage, reduce dependency on synthetic inputs, and complete the nutrient cycle. Composting animal manure can improve soil fertility and encourage the development of nutritious crops when applied to fields. The closed-loop method is a prime example of how sustainable animal husbandry is regenerative, with each part having a specific function within the more excellent ecological system.

Another critical factor in tackling the problems caused by climate change is animal husbandry. Carbon is sequestered in the soil by well-managed grazing systems, reducing greenhouse gas emissions. Animals and healthy grasslands have a symbiotic interaction that helps to store carbon and increase soil organic matter. On the other hand, industrial livestock farms that utilize concentrated feed and support deforestation frequently worsen environmental conditions and increase greenhouse gas emissions. Sustainable animal husbandry becomes an effective weapon in the battle against climate change by prioritizing pasture-based systems and regenerative approaches.

Raising animals on diverse, regenerative farms is consistent with the ideas of agroecology, which emphasize the interplay of ecological, social, and economic factors. Agroecology aims to develop robust, sustainable food systems that benefit nearby populations and increase biodiversity. Incorporating sustainable animal husbandry into agroecological farming enhances the resilience and general health of the agricultural landscape, promoting a more peaceful coexistence of human activities and the ecosystems they support.

In summary, sustainable animal husbandry is a comprehensive strategy for food production that emphasizes treating animals humanely, incorporates livestock into regenerative agricultural systems, and aims to build resilient, closed-loop ecosystems. Through pasture-based systems, varied breeds, and agroecological concepts, sustainable animal husbandry practitioners enhance the welfare of their animals and the health of the surrounding environment and the land. Sustainable animal husbandry arises as a model that aligns with the values of ecological responsibility, animal welfare, and the development of a more sustainable and regenerative food system, as consumers choose ethical and sustainable food choices.

CHAPTER VII

Off-Grid Cooking and Preservation

Outdoor Cooking Solutions

In the domain of off-grid life, where self-sufficiency and sustainability are of the utmost importance, cooking outside becomes not just a need but also a pleasant gastronomic adventure. Individuals navigating off-grid lifestyles must discover alternate and inventive ways to make meals and preserve food since they have little or no access to typical kitchen facilities. The rich tapestry of tastes that outdoor cooking offers to the off-grid table is celebrated in this section, which looks into the various outdoor cooking solutions that are in harmony with the off-grid philosophy. These solutions include everything from open-flame cooking methods to creative preservation techniques.

The open flame is a fundamental way that links folks with the real art of fire. It is also one of the oldest and most straightforward techniques of cooking outdoors. The force of flames may be harnessed in various ways, from campfires to portable fire pits, and it can lend a distinctive smokiness and depth to foods. Grilling over an open flame is a popular cooking method for people who live off the grid since it offers the ideal platform for cooking various foods, including meats and vegetables. In changing ordinary food into culinary marvels, the dance of flames provides a distinguishable taste. In addition, cooking over an open flame is a perfect fit for off-grid living since it requires very little equipment and uses renewable resources like firewood.

As a result of its longevity, adaptability, and uniform heat distribution, cast iron cookware is highly regarded as a symbol in the world of outdoor cooking. Cast iron skillets, grills, and Dutch ovens are frequently utilized by those living off the grid to prepare hearty and savory meals. Cast iron in outdoor cooking lends an air of rustic allure, whether it is elevated above an open fire or positioned on a portable grill. A wide range of recipes, from delicious stews boiling over an open flame to cornbread baking in a Dutch oven, are acceptable for using this material because of its sturdiness. The tastes of each dish are enhanced through the process of seasoning cast iron over time, resulting in the creation of a gourmet patina that tells the tale of numerous meals enjoyed around the fire.

With portable grills and outdoor cookers, off-gridders can prepare a wide range of foods quickly and efficiently while maintaining mobility and adaptability. A steady heat is provided by grills that are fuelled by propane or charcoal, making them suitable for grilling, roasting, and even baking. Portable grills transform into adaptable outdoor kitchens because they allow users to adjust the temperature and the time they cook. This gives individuals the opportunity to experiment with a wide variety of recipes and cooking techniques. Off-grid culinary experiences are given a contemporary twist by these tiny yet powerful outdoor cookers, which can be used for various cooking tasks, from searing steaks to slow-cooking casseroles.

Wood-fired ovens provide a one-of-a-kind adventure in outdoor cooking for individuals looking for a more conventional and hands-on approach. To offer a varied cooking environment, these ovens, often constructed from basic materials such as clay or brick, utilize the radiant heat generated by a wood fire. Pizzas, bread, and vegetables roasted in a wood-fired oven take on a particular flavor, which lends an air of artisanal allure to meals prepared off the grid. Off-gridders who want to establish a connection to the elemental aspect of outdoor cooking will find that fueling the fire, maintaining temperatures, and monitoring the cooking process becomes an absorbing and fulfilling culinary undertaking.

Off-grinders need help preserving food with the

assistance of contemporary refrigeration solutions, which has led to the investigation of traditional food preservation methods. In off-grid communities, smoking and dehydrating, two processes that were traditionally considered crucial for the preservation of food, are seeing a renaissance. For the goal of imparting a robust, smokey taste to meats and fish while also preserving them, smokehouses are frequently constructed using materials that have been recycled. In dehydrators, fruits, vegetables, and herbs are transformed into lightweight, shelf-stable, and delectable treats that may be enjoyed throughout the year. These dehydrators are powered by solar energy or other off-grid sources of energy. These preservation techniques lengthen the amount of time that food can be stored and bring distinctive and concentrated tastes to culinary masterpieces made off the grid.

Homeowners who live off the grid can utilize solar cooking, an environmentally friendly and energy-efficient method of preparing meals by harnessing the sun's power. The harvesting and concentrating of sunlight onto cooking vessels is the primary function of solar cookers, ranging from straightforward reflecting panel configurations to more complex parabolic concentrators. Taking this environmentally responsible technique not only reduces the amount of conventional fuel sources that are required, but it also adds a new facet to the practice of cooking outside. Solar ovens may be utilized for baking, roasting, and slow cooking to demonstrate the versatility of off-grid cooking solutions to harness renewable energy for culinary purposes.

Fermentation as a method for preserving and enriching

the tastes of off-grid meals is a time-honored practice that should be considered. Off-gridders frequently explore the realm of fermented foods, a process in which vegetables, fruits, and even drinks go through a series of transformations that release a variety of diverse tastes and nutritional advantages. Fermented veggies, such as sauerkraut and kimchi, have become indispensable cooking ingredients in off-grid kitchens because they provide a blast of acidic and probiotic-rich deliciousness. Fermented beverages, like kombucha and mead, are a great example of the inventiveness and ingenuity of off-gridders. These individuals take advantage of natural fermentation processes to create distinctive and delectable beverages.

The off-grid lifestyle, which strongly focuses on self-sufficiency and sustainability, allows cultivating a culinary landscape in which outdoor cooking solutions become an intrinsic part of everyday life. The off-grid embraces various techniques that will enable them to connect with nature and cultivate a profound love for the art of outdoor cooking. These skills include relishing the smokiness of a meal that has been grilled over an open flame, experimenting with baking in a wood-fired oven, and investigating ancient ways of food preservation. In this realm, every meal is transformed into a celebration of resourcefulness, inventiveness, and the one-of-a-kind tastes that result from the harmonious union of old knowledge and modern invention.

Canning and Food Preservation Techniques

In self-sufficiency and sustainable living, learning the skill of canning and food preservation is a cornerstone of assuring a year-round supply of produce that is either grown at home or gathered from the surrounding area. Not only can these time-honored practices lengthen the shelf life of fruits, vegetables, and other culinary gems, but they also create the opportunity for folks to experience the essence of each season for a considerable amount of time after harvesting. Individuals are given the ability to harness the richness of nature's abundance and appreciate its flavors throughout the year using this section, which discusses the many ways of canning and food preservation. These methods range from primary water bath canning to new food preservation techniques like fermentation.

Regarding food preservation, water bath canning is a time-honored technique that has been a mainstay in kitchens for many years. Fruits, tomatoes, and pickles are examples of items that are particularly well-suited to this method because of their high acidity. As part of the procedure, sealed jars are submerged in boiling water, which results in a vacuum seal that inhibits the development of bacteria that cause rotting. Heat not only guarantees that the food that has been preserved is safe to consume but also contributes to the production of tastes that are rich and brilliant colors. Water bath canning is an excellent starting point for those just beginning their journey into home preservation because it is readily available to novices and requires just a tiny amount of equipment.

Pressure canning has emerged as an essential method when preserving low-acid items, such as vegetables, meats, and legumes. In contrast to canning in a water bath, pressure canning is accomplished by utilizing high temperatures and steam pressure to remove the possibility of botulism and other hazardous microorganisms. The method involves placing jars inside a pressure canner, a specialized device that elevates the temperature inside the jars to a level higher than the boiling point of water. Through the use of this method, not only is the shelf life of a wider variety of foods increased but also the nutritional value and texture of such foods are maintained. Even though it requires specialized equipment, pressure canning is a versatile and effective method that may be used to stock the pantry with various home-preserved treats.

Individuals are rediscovering the advantages of fermented foods high in probiotics and delicious, which has led to a rise in the popularity of fermentation, an old food preservation technique. The method includes utilizing the power of helpful microbes, like lactic acid bacteria, to turn raw components into pleasures that are both tart and preserved. Vegetables, fruits, and even dairy products go through procedures that keep them and improve their nutritional profile. These processes are known as transformations. Fermented foods such as sauerkraut, kimchi, pickles, and yogurt are just a few examples of the wide variety of fermented foods that are featured on the tables of individuals who adhere to this time-honored form of sustenance preservation.

The process of dehydration is a tried-and-true method that eliminates moisture from food, preventing the growth of bacteria that cause food to go rancid and prolonging the shelf life of the food. Dehydrators provide a regulated environment for preserving fruits, vegetables, herbs, and even meats, unlike sun-drying, which is still a straightforward and natural method of drying ingredients. The elimination of water results in the concentration of tastes and nutrients, producing lightweight, shelf-stable goods that may be rehydrated for use in culinary applications. When it comes to conserving the essence of the crop, dehydration offers a diverse option that may be used for various purposes, including dried fruits for snacking and herbs for flavoring.

Root cellaring is a process that is low-tech yet very successful. It includes preserving fruits and vegetables in a cold, dark, and damp atmosphere. To establish an environment suitable for long-term storage, this method uses the natural conditions that exist underground. Historically widespread in ancient homesteads, root cellars offer an area that may be used to store different types of crops without the need for power. Some examples of these crops include potatoes, carrots, and apples. Because the mild temperatures slow the ripening process, and the high humidity prevents dehydration, folks can enjoy a consistent supply of homegrown vegetables throughout the winter months.

The incredible variety of aromas and textures that may be achieved by pickling, a method of food preservation that mixes the sourness of vinegar with the crispness of fresh vegetables, is highly satisfying. Pickling is a flexible technique that may be used to convert everyday vegetables and fruits into delicious and zesty delicacies. This technique can make chutneys, pickled beets, and traditional dill pickles. A brine solution that contains vinegar, salt, and spices is commonly used in the procedure, which entails submerging the vegetables in the brine solution. The acidity of the vinegar not only gives the pickled items their distinctive tang but also serves as a natural preservative, guaranteeing that they will last for a long time with proper storage.

A common feature of contemporary approaches to food preservation is the use of old techniques and modern perspectives. The freeze-drying process, for instance, uses cutting-edge technology to remove moisture from meals at extremely low temperatures. This process results in items that have a longer shelf life while still maintaining their nutritional content and their natural textures. This method has been used to preserve fruits, vegetables, and whole meals. It offers a handy and lightweight alternative for individuals looking for products that may be stored for an extended period without compromising on their quality.

The processes of canning and food preservation become not only valuable skills as individuals embrace the concepts of sustainable living and self-sufficiency, but they also become outlets for artistic expression and the exploration of culinary possibilities. A link to the changing seasons and the many gifts that nature bestows is reflected in the pantry, packed with jars of colorful jams, pickles, and sauces on display. The art of preservation becomes a celebration of flavors, a testament to resourcefulness, and a means of ensuring a year-round supply of nourishing and delicious food. This is true whether the preservation process is carried out by the rhythmic hum of a pressure canner, the slow transformation of fermenting vegetables, or the gentle hum of a dehydrator.

Building a Root Cellar

There is a long-standing custom of constructing root cellars, which originates from the knowledge of our predecessors who were interested in utilizing the natural cycles of the environment for preserving food. Even as we manage the complexity of contemporary living, the time-honored technique of building a root cellar continues to serve as a shining example of simplicity and sustainability. Extending the shelf life of fruits, vegetables, and other perishable items can be accomplished by utilizing this underground storage area, typically located beneath the earth's surface. The purpose of this investigation is to look into the art of building a root cellar, revealing its historical significance, the science behind its construction, and the practical processes involved in establishing a sanctuary for the wealth that nature provides.

Root cellars have a long and storied history intricately woven into the fabric of human history. The necessity of storing food beyond the harvest season was something that our predecessors understood when they lived in different civilizations and on other continents. Agricultural communities are characterized by a strong sense of collective knowledge, which is demonstrated by the fact that the construction of root cellars was a communal activity. Communities could bridge the gap between abundance and famine by utilizing these underground buildings, which acted as nutrition stores. Root cellars were a concrete link to the cyclical rhythm of planting, harvesting, and storing food. They reflected a harmonious relationship with nature and provided a tangible connection to the cycle.

The effective operation of a root cellar depends on a comprehensive grasp of the natural laws that govern it. These buildings are usually positioned below the frost line, approximately 8 to 10 feet. They use the consistent warmth of the soil to produce a climate that is perfect for food storage. Root cellars capitalize on the coldness of the ground to slow down the ripening and decay processes by maintaining a temperature range between 32 degrees Fahrenheit and 40 degrees Fahrenheit (0 degrees Celsius and 4 degrees Celsius). The high humidity levels within the basement prevent the fruits and vegetables from dehydrating, which helps ensure they stay fresh.

A root cellar's success depends on its construction because of its strategic placement within the natural environment. Choosing a high location helps prevent water from pooling, and situating it close to the homestead offers increased convenience. Because it maintains a more consistent temperature, the north side of a hill is frequently preferred among people. It is of the utmost importance to give careful thought to soil drainage to avoid waterlogging. Additionally, the entry should be oriented away from the predominant winds to reduce temperature swings. Placing a root cellar in such a way that it is in harmony with the natural contours of the ground makes it an essential component of the ecosystem.

The building of a root cellar provides an opportunity for creative expression by enabling the use of a wide range of materials and approaches to design. Construction may be done using wood, concrete, or earthbags, all of which are typical alternatives, and each has its own set of benefits. A classic appearance is imparted by wood, although the resilience of concrete is not compromised. Construction using earthbags, which consist of many layers of earth-filled bags, is consistent with environmentally responsible building standards. Insulating the building is one design factor that helps manage temperature successfully. Whether the construction is rectangular, circular, or a modified Quonset hut, it should be able to blend in perfectly with the natural environment when it is constructed.

The construction of a root cellar is a labor-intensive project that requires careful design and execution before completion. A primary subterranean storage facility can be constructed by following the processes outlined in the following paragraphs.

To begin the procedure, excavate the selected spot to the needed depth with the appropriate equipment. An eight to ten feet below the earth's surface is often enough. Put the floor on a level surface and ensure adequate drainage to prevent water from pooling.

To construct the walls, use the materials that have been selected, and if required, reinforce them with support beams. To the individual's preferences, the shape may be rectangular, circular, or a modified version of the Quonset hut design. It is possible to change the temperature by incorporating insulation into the walls.

Ventilation is an essential component to facilitate air circulation within the root cellar. Installing pipes or vents that extend above ground is one method that can be utilized to accomplish this goal. Using mesh screens allows for adequate ventilation while simultaneously preventing the ingress of pests.

Shelving systems should be installed to help arrange and separate the many sorts of produce. It is essential to maximize the use of space, and shelves that are thoughtfully constructed guarantee that there is sufficient ventilation around the goods that are being kept.

To prevent temperature swings, the roof needs to be adequately insulated. Insulation materials commonly used include straw bales, foam boards, and other more suited solutions. A sturdy roof substantially improves the efficiency of the cellar as a whole.

Create a safe entry that reduces the amount of heat that is transferred. Keeping the temperature within the root cellar constant is made more accessible by having an entryway that slopes downward and a door that opens inward.

Variations of root cellars include a cold storage pit within the building itself. This bottom compartment provides more flexibility in food preservation by allowing for storing things that are more suited to somewhat colder temperatures.

In addition to the immediate preservation of food, the building and operation of root cellars result in many advantages that extend beyond the conservation of meals. Root cellars are a living space that exemplifies a self-sufficient and environmentally conscious way of life, perfectly harmonious with the ideals of homesteading and off-grid living.

An essential function of a root cellar is to act as a bridge between time and space, enabling folks to continue to enjoy the results of their work long after the growing season has come to an end. Root cellars can successfully increase the shelf life of homegrown fruit because they are designed to create a climate that is more similar to the chilly and damp temperatures that are present in nature.

As an alternative to contemporary refrigeration, root cellars are an energy-efficient solution since they do not require electricity. This is consistent with the concepts of off-grid living, which include increasing self-sufficiency and limiting reliance on conventional equipment.

The fact that root cellars are not harmful to the environment is one factor that contributes to their sustainability. It is possible for individuals to actively decrease their ecological footprint and battle the severe issue of food waste by reducing the need for refrigeration and preventing food from going rancid.

Developing a solid connection to the natural world can be accomplished by constructing and utilizing a root cellar. The comprehension of seasonal cycles, the significance of preparation, and the rhythmic dance of nature's abundance are encouraged. Not only does this relationship extend beyond the practical concerns of food preservation, but it also fosters a sense of harmony with the surrounding environment.

Even if building root cellars together as a community may be less common today, community involvement is still alive. Even when a single person makes them, root cellars represent a common belief in the need to be prepared and live sustainably. The information and abilities linked with root cellars may be shared throughout communities, providing a sense of community and solidarity.

Creating a root cellar will emerge as a thread connecting the past, the present, and the future in the rich tapestry of sustainable living. In addition to representing a return to simplicity, it also represents a dedication to self-reliance and a harmonious dance with the rhythms of nature. In addition to preserving food, root cellars are a repository of ageless knowledge passed down from generation to generation. The bare root cellar encourages us to rediscover the lasting significance of traditions and the sustainable practices ingrained in our collective past as we traverse an era characterized by technological breakthroughs. With the construction of a root cellar, we can ensure that we will have food to eat and a more profound awareness of the complex relationship between humans and the natural world.

CHAPTER VIII

Thriving with Off-Grid Technology

Off-Grid Internet and Communication

As we live in an era dominated by digital contact and connection, the possibility of adopting an off-grid lifestyle presents a set of obstacles that are unparalleled in maintaining connectivity. Even though disengaging from the traditional power grid and embracing a self-sufficient way of life is appealing, the requirement for dependable off-grid internet and communication solutions is becoming increasingly apparent. This section aims to investigate the nexus between self-sufficiency and digital communication by delving into the many techniques, technologies, and concerns necessary for sustaining a semblance of connectedness in the off-grid area.

An individual interested in off-grid living is confronted with a contradictory situation: the desire to be alone in a natural setting conflicts with the requirement to maintain a connection to the computer world. The search for off-grid internet solutions becomes an essential component when it comes to bringing together contemporary connections and an independent way of life. This is true whether the requirement is for business, unexpected crises, or the simple desire to obtain information and enjoyment.

Satellite internet has emerged as a critical player in off-grid connectivity. It provides coverage in remote areas where traditional wired or wireless services fall short. Using satellites orbiting the Earth, users can access the internet almost anywhere, provided they have a clear view of the sky. However, satellite internet has drawbacks, including latency issues and data limitations. These constraints can make it less suitable for bandwidth-intensive activities like online gaming or video streaming.

Off-grid communication can be accomplished through the use of mesh networks, which promote decentralization and collaboration. Mesh networks are characterized by the presence of linked nodes that are able to interact with one another. Mesh networks may be built with a wide range of devices, ranging from specialized mesh routers to smartphones that have been repurposed. Users can establish a local network with the help of this autonomous system, making it possible for devices to communicate with one another even without conventional internet infrastructure. Mesh networks can flourish on the principles of resilience and adaptation, making them excellent for communities that are not connected to the grid and distant regions that do not have centralized communication infrastructure.

Ham radio, also known as amateur radio, is a solid off-grid communication option that has been around for a long time and has proven robust. It allows for reliable communication over vast distances without standard networks. By utilizing radio frequencies designated for amateur usage, licensed operators can send not just voice but data and even pictures. Ham radio technology, which can range from portable transceivers to complex base stations, makes it possible for off-gridders to communicate with the ham radio community worldwide and, more crucially, with local users in the surrounding neighborhood. This decentralized and autonomous communication style is instrumental in times of emergency when standard communication routes may fail to convey information effectively.

Utilizing communication equipment not connected to the grid frequently entails optimizing energy use to conform to the principles of self-sufficiency. Solar-powered chargers, portable generators, and energy-efficient gadgets are essential for off-grid communication setups. To preserve the connection, providing a dependable power supply is of the utmost importance, particularly in off-grid territories where conventional electrical grids are inaccessible.

Off-grinders can sustainably power their communication equipment by using renewable energy sources, reducing their impact on the environment.

There has been an increase in the number of inventive solutions adapted to the specific requirements of individuals who are interested in living a self-sufficient lifestyle due to the convergence of off-grid living and current communication technology. Off-grid-friendly smartphones are designed to meet the needs of users who place a high priority on connectivity without sacrificing the ruggedness that is necessary for off-grid excursions. These smartphones are equipped with energy-efficient features and sturdy designs, respectively. Additionally, these devices typically come with specific applications that allow offline navigation, emergency communication, and access to vital information, even when internet connectivity is spotty.

To strike a healthy balance between the concepts of sustainability and the need for connectivity, the off-grid lifestyle requires a careful attitude. It is necessary to be ready to adjust to the constraints inherent in living in a remote location to embrace off-grid internet and communication options. Although satellite internet, mesh networks, and ham radio provide customers with various alternatives, they must consider the trade-offs in terms of speed, dependability, and energy usage throughout their decision-making process. Individuals modify their communication tactics to correspond with their requirements and the requirements of their chosen off-grid living as they discover off-grid connectivity, which becomes a voyage of inquiry and experimentation.

It is optional to completely disengage from the interconnected world to pursue an off-grid living in this day and age of digital technology. The alternative is that it encourages individuals to traverse the digital wilderness with intention, using new solutions to keep a meaningful connection with the larger community. The junction between off-grid life and current communication technology represents a peaceful coexistence. This is where the virtues of self-sufficiency meet the developing needs of a connected world, enabling individuals to carve out their own route within the enormous expanse of off-grid living.

Sustainable Gadgets and Appliances

Throughout the rapid development of technology, there is a rising awareness of the importance of sustainability, which is transforming the landscape of electronic devices and home appliances. As more and more people become aware of the critical need for environmentally responsible behaviors, there has been an increase in the demand for environmentally friendly alternatives to electronic gadgets. This section dives into the rapidly expanding field of environmentally friendly devices and appliances. It examines how technological advancement and ecological awareness come together to provide solutions that reduce their negative influence on the environment without sacrificing their functioning.

Energy efficiency is one of the most critical factors for environmentally friendly devices. Smart home gadgets, which include anything from lighting systems to thermostats, have transitioned to reduce the amount of energy consumed. Manufacturers have been motivated to create devices and appliances that fulfill high energy efficiency criteria due to the introduction of Energy Star and other eco-certifications. In the case of smart thermostats, for example, they intelligently adjust heating and cooling depending on consumption patterns, maximizing energy use and lowering the total impact on the environment.

Solar-powered devices have emerged as a shining example of environmentally responsible innovation. These devices use the sun's plentiful energy to power various electronic devices. Solar chargers, for example, provide a portable and sustainable energy source that may be used to charge tiny electronic devices such as laptops, cellphones, and other similar gadgets. Solar-powered lighting solutions can be used not only for charging but also to brighten houses and outdoor areas without relying on traditional power plants. Incorporating solar technology into commonplace electronic devices signifies a paradigm shift toward lessening reliance on limited energy supplies.

Because the problem of electronic waste constitutes a massive threat to the environment, the creation of devices that are meant to be long-lasting, upgradeable, and recyclable has been prompted. Modular cell phones, for instance, allow customers to update or replace particular components without throwing away the entire device. To encourage the recycling of components and lessen the negative impact that electronic waste has on the environment, manufacturers are progressively embracing designs that make it as simple as possible to disassemble their products.

The Internet of Things (IoT) has been an essential component in developing more environmentally friendly and innovative houses. Users can monitor and regulate their energy use, keep track of the resources they consume, and maximize their household equipment's overall efficiency through smart home ecosystems. Smart refrigerators that reduce food waste by tracking inventory and intelligent lighting systems that change brightness based on the amount of natural light present are two examples of devices enabled by the Internet of Things (IoT) that contribute to the establishment of environmentally aware living spaces.

To reduce the environmental impact of electronic devices, efforts are being made to reduce the amount of materials utilized in their manufacturing. Environmentally friendly materials, such as bamboo, recycled plastics, and biodegradable chemicals, are becoming increasingly popular in producing electronic gadgets. An example of a dedication to lowering the environmental effect of electronic manufacturing is the production of environmentally friendly laptops and cell phones. These products are made from recycled aluminum and components that are sourced responsibly.

The utilization of ambient energy sources to power devices is an innovative approach to developing environmentally friendly gadgets represented by energy harvesting technology. Power generation for tiny electronic devices may be accomplished by utilizing kinetic energy, thermal differentials, and radio frequency signals, among other sources. From self-charging watches that catch kinetic energy from wrist movements to radio frequency identification (RFID) tags that fuel themselves due to ambient radio waves, energy harvesting offers promise for developing electronic devices that have a decreased reliance on conventional power sources.

Environmentally friendly home appliances go beyond technology and include things like washing machines, refrigerators, and water heaters, including those critical to the family. Energy-efficient appliances, characterized by high Energy Star ratings, can save monthly power costs and contribute to more significant sustainability initiatives in the energy sector. An excellent example of incorporating environmentally friendly technology into commonplace household appliances is the development of heat pump water heaters, which can warm water by drawing heat from the surrounding air.

There has been a movement in consumer ideals toward living more environmentally responsible, which is reflected in the proliferation of sustainable electronics and appliances. As people grow more conscious of their impact on the environment, there has been an increase in the demand for products that align with these ideals, which has led to innovation across all sectors of the economy. In recent years, the circular economy model has gained popularity as a sustainable approach to the consumption of electronic goods. This model emphasizes the longevity, repairability, and recycling of products. Within the consumer electronics sector, a growing culture of sustainability is being fostered by manufacturers who are progressively accepting responsibility for the whole lifespan of their goods, beginning with creation and ending with disposal.

To summarize, the development of environmentally friendly electrical appliances and devices is a prime example of how technological advancement and environmental consciousness may harmoniously coexist. The field of electronics is currently undertaking a revolutionary journey towards reducing its influence on the environment. This journey includes technological advancements such as solar-powered inventions and energy-efficient intelligent gadgets. Manufacturers are driven to seek new solutions that not only satisfy functional demands but also contribute to a more sustainable and peaceful cohabitation with the earth because customers are placing a greater emphasis on sustainability in their purchasing decisions. It is a communal commitment to promoting a greener, more sustainable future where technology acts as a catalyst for good environmental change, and the incorporation of eco- wisdom into the world of gadgets and appliances reflects this dedication.

Integrating Smart Solutions in Remote Living

As technology continues to evolve rapidly, it reshapes the concept of remote living, introducing ingenious solutions that enhance both sustainability and comfort. Whether residing in rural houses, distant cottages, or off-grid homesteads, innovative technology empowers individuals to tackle the challenges of isolation while maintaining a harmonious relationship with the environment. This section explores the diverse ways these innovative solutions are revolutionizing remote living, ushering in a new era where sustainability, efficiency, and connectivity converge to redefine the possibilities for independent living.

Energy management is one of the main pillars of intelligent solutions for remote living. Residents can effectively monitor and control their energy use with the help of intelligent off-grid systems that are outfitted with sophisticated energy monitoring and optimization features. By combining solar charge controllers, energy storage devices, and smart inverters, users may efficiently utilize renewable energy sources and guarantee a steady electricity supply even without conventional electrical networks. People may modify their energy consumption habits to maximize effectiveness and reduce waste using remote control and real-time monitoring features. This aligns with the sustainability ideals of living in a distant location.

Home automation plays a crucial role in enhancing the security and convenience of remote homes. Residents can manage their homes from afar, thanks to the remote monitoring and control features of smart thermostats, lighting systems, and security cameras. These innovative solutions not only help to cut down on energy costs but also provide a sense of security and peace of mind by automating lighting schedules based on occupancy, remotely activating security systems, and adjusting the temperature before guests arrive. They also help to mitigate some of the challenges associated with remote living.

Connectivity is a defining characteristic of modern life, and the use of intelligent communication technology has become indispensable in remote settings. Remote residents can maintain connections with the outside world thanks to off-grid communication options like mesh networks and satellite internet, bridging the gap between isolation and connectedness. Smartphones are vital tools for navigating the wilderness and staying connected with friends, family, and emergency services; equipped with offline navigation apps and emergency communication features. Off-grid living and intelligent communication technology converge to offer a sophisticated solution that preserves the solitude of remote places while fostering essential connections to the broader world community.

Managing water is essential in isolated situations that significantly benefit from clever solutions. Water use may be effectively monitored and controlled with the help of intelligent water systems, which come with sensors and automation functions. These technologies help to preserve this valuable resource, from rainwater harvesting systems that automatically redirect collected rainwater to irrigation when needed to intelligent leak detection systems that notify users of possible water waste. The use of bright water solutions fits with the principles of sustainability and self-sufficiency in rural living, where access to water may be restricted.

Innovative technology has made precision agriculture possible, and it is now essential to isolated homesteads and rural life. Precision farming and resource optimization are made possible by the increased efficiency of agricultural techniques brought about by intelligent sensors, drones, and automated farm equipment. These technologies, which range from smart tractors with GPS-guided precision farming capabilities to soil moisture sensors that influence irrigation decisions, enable people living in distant areas to optimize agricultural output while reducing environmental damage.

Living remotely significantly impacts one's health and well-being, and creative solutions support both proactive and reactive healthcare. People may measure their vital signs and get real-time feedback on their well-being with wearables with health monitoring functions. When smart gadgets are combined with remote health monitoring systems, prompt medical treatments and consultations are possible, which lessens the difficulties in getting healthcare services in remote places. Integrating smart technology and healthcare in remote settings encourages a comprehensive approach to well-being.

Smart waste management methods are essential to keep distant living places clean and environmentally intact. By optimizing garbage collection schedules depending on fill levels, smart bins with sensors can reduce pointless trips and the carbon footprint associated with waste disposal.

Recycling programs aided by intelligent sorting technology can promote sustainable waste management techniques in remote locations. There are difficulties in integrating smart technologies with remote life. Connectivity, power consumption, and dependence on electronic systems are issues that need to be carefully considered and tailored to the particularities of distant situations. Privacy concerns often surface as people try to balance the need for privacy in remote life and smart technology.

To sum up, incorporating intelligent solutions into distant living signifies a paradigm change that enables people to surmount the obstacles of being alone while embracing efficiency and sustainability. Smart technologies improve rural living standards through energy management, communication, agriculture, and healthcare. With these technologies still developing, remote living might eventually cohabit peacefully with the environment, pushing the limits of independent living to new heights as efficiency and connectedness come together. Technology is an enabler in the smart remote living period, promoting self-sufficiency, resilience, and a close bond with the natural world and the global community.

CHAPTER IX

Wellness and Self-Care Off the Grid

Designing a Homestead Wellness Routine

The notion of a homestead wellness routine arises as a holistic approach to harmonizing physical, mental, and emotional well-being within the tranquility of country living. This concept emerges in the middle of the rush and bustle of modern life. The process of developing a wellness routine on a farm extends beyond the boundaries of conventional exercise routines; it involves establishing a mutually beneficial relationship with the natural environment, which helps to cultivate a feeling of equilibrium, resilience, and sustainable health practices. In this section, the fundamental components of developing a homestead wellness routine are investigated. Particular attention is paid to the incorporation of mindful living, physical exercise, nutrition, and connection with environment in order to foster a lifestyle that is both thriving and sustainable.

Individuals are encouraged to be present and aware of their daily activities through mindful living, which is the fundamental pillar of a household health regimen. Mindfulness takes on a distinct personality when practiced amid the peace and quiet of a farm, which encourages a more profound connection with the world's natural cycles. Individuals can build a heightened awareness of their environment, which may foster a sense of thankfulness and presence. This can be accomplished through morning meditation sessions and thoughtful walks through the farm. The practice of mindful living on a farm extends to the chores that are performed daily, so converting mundane activities into occasions for introspection and appreciation of the natural environment.

When it comes to a homestead health regimen, physical exercise takes on a different form. This is because it incorporates functional motions with the requirements of rural living. The activities that are performed on a homestead, such as gardening, tending to livestock, and construction projects, naturally include physical exercise into the daily routine. Not only does this integration improve cardiovascular health and strength, but it also instills a profound feeling of purpose and achievement in the individual's mind. The sense of accomplishment from these activities is unparalleled. Aside from that, engaging in sports like hiking, trail running, and yoga while surrounded by the natural sceneries of the homestead is beneficial to both the physical fitness of the individual and the mental renewal of the individual.

When living on a homestead, nutrition becomes an essential component of overall health, emphasizing the production and consumption of fresh produce that is acquired locally. Cultivating one's fruits and vegetables instills a sense of connection with the soil and encourages the consumption of a diet that is abundant in nutrients. Individuals collect the fruits of their work and engage in meal preparation with an emphasis on whole, unprocessed foods, which leads to the development of farm-to-table activities as a way of life. The significance of providing the body with healthful and environmentally responsible options is brought to light through the symbiotic relationship between nutrition and farmstead living.

A homestead health regimen should always include a connection with nature as an essential component. This connection provides therapeutic advantages that go beyond the world of the physical. Spending time outside, whether in the garden, by the stream, or beneath the shade of old trees, is a revitalizing practice. The cultivation of a strong sense of awe and connection with the natural world can be accomplished through activities such as stargazing, birding, and nature walks that take place under clear sky. Through alleviating stress, enhancing mood, and cultivating a profound sense of well-being, this relationship with nature acts as a salve for the soul.

Practices such as journaling, creative expression, and community interaction are examples of activities that are included in the homestead wellness routine. These activities expand the routine's reach into mental and emotional health. Journaling transforms into a reflecting tool that may be used to explore ideas and feelings, therefore recording the one-of-a-kind experiences that come with living on a farm. Whether it be via the medium of painting, music, or crafts, creative activities offer opportunities for self-expression and stress reduction simultaneously. A feeling of belonging and emotional resilience are fostered via community participation on a homestead, which frequently takes the form of collaborative projects, gatherings of the community, and the development of a network of people who support one another.

A homestead that takes a holistic approach to well-being recognizes the significance of a well-rested body and mind, and one of the components of this approach is getting enough rest and sleep. The natural rhythms of the homestead, which are affected by dawn and sunset, provide an atmosphere conducive to establishing good sleep habits. Deep, restful sleep is promoted by disconnecting from technological gadgets and enjoying the stillness of rural nights. This contributes to an overall improvement in well-being on a more fundamental level.

A consciousness of environmentally responsible behaviors becomes of the utmost importance when individuals develop their wellness regimen. Wellness and environmental stewardship may be aligned by implementing environmentally responsible choices, such as composting, water conservation, and energy-efficient devices. The overall well-being created by a homestead wellness practice is delicately woven into the fabric of sustainable living, highlighting the interdependence of health on an individual level and the environment's vitality.

In conclusion, developing a wellness routine for the homestead encompasses a multifaceted approach to well-being that goes beyond the paradigms of conventional exercise. A comprehensive pattern for flourishing on a farm is created when mindful living, physical exercise integrated with everyday duties, nutritional food, connection with nature, and mental and emotional involvement all come together. This wellness regimen not only adds to the overall sustainability and resilience of the homestead environment but also helps boost the health of individuals who participate in it. In the process of embracing the rhythms of rural living, individuals begin on a journey toward a balanced, lively, sustainable lifestyle that is in harmony with the natural environment.

Natural Remedies and Herbalism

In the ever-changing world of wellness, the resurgence of interest in natural remedies and herbalism is a tribute to humanity's continuing connection with the healing capabilities of the plant kingdom. Herbal medicine and natural remedies are two examples of this vital link. Herbalism, which originates in ancient customs and folk wisdom, is a practice that transcends cultural boundaries and provides a holistic approach to health and well-being. This section goes into natural medicines and herbalism, examining the historical context, principles, and present significance of these practices in fostering physical, mental, and emotional vigor from a holistic perspective.

A close connection may be between herbalism's history and human civilization's development. Ancient communities have recognized plants' healing potential and established complex systems of herbal medicine. These societies have been found across a variety of cultures and continents. There is a rich tapestry of knowledge surrounding the use of plants for medical purposes that various cultures have produced. Some examples of these cultures are Ayurveda in India, Traditional Chinese Medicine, Native American botanical traditions, and European herbal traditions. The remarkable influence that nature's pharmacopeia has on human health is demonstrated by the fact that these traditions, frequently handed down from generation to generation, served as the foundation of early healthcare systems.

The underlying premise underpinning herbalism is that plants contain a wide variety of chemicals that can be used for therapeutic purposes. There are various complicated ways in which the active ingredients found in herbs interact with the body. These interactions help to correct imbalances and assist the body's natural healing processes. A holistic approach is utilized by herbalists, which considers the symptoms and the individual's constitution, lifestyle, and environment alongside the symptoms. This individualized approach aligns with the more general notion of holistic health, which recognizes the interdependence of a person's physical, mental, and emotional well-being.

In recent decades, there has been a resurgence of interest in herbalism. This enthusiasm has been spurred partly by a greater understanding of the limits and adverse effects of various pharmacological approaches. The efficacy of many traditional herbal treatments has been validated by scientific studies, which has contributed to the illumination of the biochemical pathways responsible for their therapeutic effects. The phytochemistry survey involves investigating plants' chemical makeup to elucidate the complex interactions between certain chemicals and their physiological effects. The convergence of conventional medical knowledge and contemporary scientific research has resulted in the development of evidence-based herbal medicine, which has contributed to incorporating herbal medicines into traditional medical procedures.

Herbal medicine comprises a wide variety of plants, each of which possesses a unique set of medicinal qualities. The herbal pharmacopeia targets a wide range of health issues, including adaptogenic herbs that help the body improve its reaction to stress, such as ashwagandha and rhodiola, as well as immune-boosting herbs, such as echinacea and elderberry. In addition, herbs such as chamomile and valerian provide natural remedies for sleep support, while ginger and peppermint are helpful for digestive disorders. Herbal medicines may also be used topically, and calendula and aloe vera are two examples of well-known plants for their ability to cure the skin.

As more people get interested in herbalism, there has been a resurgence in the importance of using environmentally responsible methods for growing and harvesting medicinal herbs. To preserve the ecological equilibrium of plant ecosystems, it is essential to practice ethical wildcrafting, adhere to permaculture principles, and use organic agricultural practices. The cultivation of herbs responsibly assures that both the current generation and future generations will be able to reap the benefits of the therapeutic richness that nature provides without jeopardizing the delicate balance among plant communities.

One of the advantages of herbalism is that it can give people more control over their health path. Learning about medicinal plants helps individuals develop a feeling of self-reliance, enabling them to take an active role in their health and wellness. Herbal medicines frequently go beyond only relieving symptoms; they also target the underlying imbalances that are considered to be contributors to health problems. This empowerment aligns with the more significant trend toward individualized and preventative approaches to healthcare, which emphasizes proactive self-care behaviors.

Even though herbalism has many advantages, it is full of difficulties. Several continuing issues must be considered when incorporating herbal medicines into modern healthcare. These include the standardization of herbal preparations, the guarantees of quality control, and the resolution of potential herb-drug interactions. In addition, it is necessary to use discretion while interpreting the vast amount of material accessible on herbal medicine because not all claims are supported by substantial examples of scientific data. Education and collaboration between herbalists, healthcare practitioners, and researchers are necessary when cultivating a well-rounded and well-informed approach to herbalism.

Herbalism is seeing a renaissance worldwide, which presents a chance for appreciation and the interchange of ideas across different cultures. The use of traditional herbal knowledge from many regions of the world adds to an approach to wellness that is both varied and inclusive. Preserving cultural traditions facilitates the smooth incorporation of herbalism within the framework of contemporary medical treatment, the recognition of indigenous knowledge, and the implementation of ethical business practices in the international herbal trade.

Natural medicines and herbalism are perfect examples of the tremendous synergy between old knowledge and modern thinking. Herbal medicine is a vibrant and ever-evolving profession within holistic health due to its historical origins, fundamental principles, and wide range of applications. In the process of individuals, healthcare practitioners, and researchers working together to investigate the possibilities of medicinal plants, herbalism continues to weave itself into the fabric of well-being. It provides a natural and sustainable method for nourishing the body, mind, and soul. Humanity goes on a voyage of rediscovery to create a closer connection with the curative power of nature via the cultivation and appreciation of herbal traditions.

Mental Health Practices in Isolation

It is important to note that the experience of solitude, whether it is a choice or forced, has significant repercussions for one's mental health. The possibility of spending lengthy amounts of time alone can elicit a wide range of sensations in a world that is defined by continual connectedness. These feelings vary from feelings of loneliness and vulnerability to feelings of reflection and self-discovery. This section aims to investigate the dynamics of mental health in solitude, diving into the problems it brings and providing insights into successful practices that encourage resilience, self-care, and psychological happiness.

There are many different ways that Isolation can show itself, including purposeful retreats for self-reflection and conditions such as quarantine or social distancing techniques. The individual's personality, the experiences they have had in the past, and the environment in which they exist all have a role in shaping their subjective feeling of Isolation. Some people may find peace and creativity in solitude, but others may struggle with feelings of Isolation, which can lead to difficulties with mental health. To build successful coping techniques, it is essential to have a thorough understanding of this complex terrain.

When it comes to mental health, Isolation may either exacerbate pre-existing problems or lead to the development of new difficulties. Feelings of loneliness, anxiety, and despair may become more intense when there is little opportunity for social connection. The lack of regularity and stimulation from the outside world might affect sleep patterns and increase stress levels. Individuals who spend lengthy time alone may confront unresolved thoughts and feelings, necessitating a careful balance between self-reflection and self-compassion.

Creating a disciplined routine might act as a stabilizing anchor in the sea of uncertainty frequently brought about by individual Isolation. Predictability and purpose are provided by a daily schedule, which helps to alleviate emotions of aimlessness and offers a sense of purpose. Incorporating activities that give joy and a feeling of achievement, such as participating in artistic endeavors, acquiring new skills, or engaging in physical activity, helps to a positive mentality focused on achieving goals. Not only does routine help maintain mental health, but it also improves one's perspective of time, which in turn makes it easier to deal with feelings of loneliness.

The discipline of mindfulness, which originates in activities like meditation and deep breathing, has revealed itself to be an effective instrument for traversing the emotional landscape of solitude. A compassionate understanding of oneself may be developed via mindful awareness, which teaches individuals to notice their thoughts and feelings without judgment. When dealing with stresses caused by Isolation, cultivating mindfulness can help reduce the adverse effects of rumination and concern, fostering a sense of calm and resilience.

Utilizing virtual platforms becomes essential in reducing Isolation's social elements in our period, which is characterized by the predominance of digital connectivity. Engaging in meaningful connections with friends, family, and support networks may be made more accessible via video chats, online communities, and social media. Maintaining social links, even in a virtual arena, helps to contribute to a sense of belonging and combats the emotions of loneliness that are caused by Isolation. Crossing physical distances and developing a feeling of community via creative collaborations, virtual events, and shared experiences on the internet is possible.

Personally, Isolation provides a one-of-a-kind chance for introspection and development of one's character. Participating in reflective practices, such as keeping a diary, allows individuals to investigate their feelings and ideas. You may establish a feeling of purpose and achievement by setting personal goals and ambitions for self-improvement. These goals and aspirations might be in skill development, hobbies, or activities promoting self-care. Taking this time alone and viewing it as a trip that might bring about change can help one develop a more optimistic outlook on the opportunities for personal development.

A caring attitude toward oneself is required to overcome loneliness, an everyday companion in Isolation. One of the most critical aspects of self-compassion is recognizing and accepting one's emotions without passing judgment on them. The emotional toll that loneliness can take can be mitigated by engaging in activities that offer delight, performing self-care practices, and creating expectations that are in keeping with reality. Individuals can negotiate these sensations with better resilience when they have the wisdom to recognize that experiencing feelings of loneliness is sometimes a natural part of the human experience.

The arts, which comprise a wide range of creative expressions ranging from writing and painting to music and dance, are potent avenues for expressing emotions when practiced in solitude. Participating in artistic activities offers a window of opportunity for the processing of feelings, the promotion of self-discovery, and the transcendence of the limitations imposed by physical confinement. In times of solitude, individuals can externalize their internal worlds and discover meaning via creative expression, which functions as a healing mechanism.

It is essential to identify situations in which solitude has a detrimental influence on mental health. Individuals seeking professional help through teletherapy or virtual counseling sessions may get coping methods, emotional validation, and a friendly environment to explore their experiences. Professions in the field of mental health provide individualized counseling to meet each individual's requirements, addressing the specific issues brought about by Isolation and encouraging psychological well-being.

In conclusion, a nuanced and proactive strategy is required to successfully navigate the landscape of mental health when functioning in Isolation. The development of a disciplined routine, the cultivation of mindfulness, the utilization of virtual connections, and the practice of self-reflection are all potent tools that may be utilized to create resilience and increase well-being. Individuals can convert moments of solitude into transformational journeys when they acknowledge the difficulties associated with Isolation while simultaneously welcoming possibilities for personal development. When faced with adversity, the human spirit's ability to adjust, acquire new knowledge, and flourish demonstrates the resiliency inherent in the quest for mental health and well-being.

CHAPTER X

Crafting and Artisanal Living

Homestead Crafts and DIY Projects

The homestead is a great place for creativity and hands-on learning because of its self-sufficient and earth-connected attitude. A self-sufficient home's utility is improved by homestead crafts and do-it-yourself projects, which also exemplify the values of resourcefulness and skill mastery. These projects enhance homesteaders' sense of success and strengthen their bond with the homestead lifestyle, from handcrafted necessities to creative manifestations of their individuality. This section examines the diverse array of homestead crafts and do-it-yourself projects, examining their importance, diversity, and all-encompassing advantages for homesteaders.

Crafts on the homestead are more than just recreational activities; they are essential to the lifestyle. These crafts are a way to become self-sufficient since they are based on pragmatism and necessity. Essentials like textiles, candles, and soap can be manufactured by hand to satisfy immediate requirements and provide an alternative to store-bought items. Crafts from the farm become a form of expression beyond practicality, exhibiting the homesteader's individuality and inventiveness as the focal point of their dwelling.

Self-sufficiency is one of the central tenets of homestead life, and making necessities is a vital part of getting there. The craft of creating soap, for example, turns ordinary components like oils and lye into an essential tool for personal hygiene. A different kind of light source may be formed by making candles out of recyclable materials or beeswax, particularly in off-grid environments. In addition to lessening the homesteader's environmental impact, these handmade necessities also give them pleasure in producing the everyday necessities they use.

Fiber arts and textiles are fields that homesteaders frequently find themselves exploring. These skills introduce the homesteader to long-standing handicraft practices, from spinning yarn and weaving textiles to making quilts and carpets. An extra layer of sustainability is added to textile projects by raising animals for wool or growing plants for natural dyes. In addition to being functional, the finished handwoven textiles tell the tale of the farm and the labor-intensive process involved in making them.

The homestead needs ongoing upkeep and growth because it is a dynamic organism. As a result, homesteaders need to be proficient in carpentry and construction. Both practical problem-solving and artistic vision are required when creating furniture, animal shelters, or buildings such as chicken coops. The capacity of the homesteader to repurpose unfinished materials into practical constructions is a prime example of the values of independence and fortitude in the face of difficulty.

Homestead crafts offer a platform for artistic expression in addition to their practical uses. A personal touch may be added to the homestead with decorative pieces like reused metal sculptures, mosaic stepping stones, and hand-painted signage. In addition to enhancing the living area, artistic pursuits show off the homesteader's individual aesthetic preferences and relationship to the land. Homestead crafts provide a creative outlet that transforms the dwelling into a visually stunning and inspiring space.

A center for culinary arts, the kitchen is the heart of the farm. Harvesting, canning, fermenting, and storing vegetables are ancient practices that guarantee a plentiful crop all year. Preparing your jams, pickles, and fermented treats increases the harvest's usefulness and yields distinctive, tasty products. Crafting in the kitchen becomes an artistic and practical way to celebrate the season's bounty.

Homestead crafts are about more than simply the finished item; they represent an ongoing knowledge acquisition and skill improvement process. Every project provides a chance for learning and development, whether learning the craft of blacksmithing, becoming an expert potter, or experimenting with natural colors. A strong sense of competence and self-efficacy is fostered by the actual skills that farmstead crafts teach, which go beyond theoretical understanding.

Among homesteaders, crafts are another vital aspect of community development. Homesteading communities benefit from the information, skills, and handcrafted items shared among community members. Mutual support and exchange of experiences may be fostered through workshops, skill-sharing sessions, and cooperative initiatives. Making things together creates unity and turns the homestead into a center of shared creation.

Homesteading is a holistic endeavor that benefits the homesteader in ways that go beyond material gains from crafts and do-it-yourself projects. Working with your hands is contemplative, which lowers stress and increases mindfulness. A person's sense of success and self-worth is increased when they create something with their hands. Grounding the homesteader in a larger historical context, the connection to traditional crafts also promotes a commitment to legacy and cultural continuity.

To sum up, homestead crafts and do-it-yourself projects are essential to the homesteader lifestyle. These crafts embody the spirit of independence, inventiveness, and a deep connection to the land, from the usefulness of handcrafted necessities to the creative expressions that beautify the farm. Homesteading is a rich and rewarding experience because of homestead crafts' holistic, educational, and social advantages. Homesteaders who uphold the value of craftsmanship not only improve the usability of their living areas but also foster a resilient, sustainable lifestyle centered around the ageless delight of making things with one's hands.

Turning Hobbies into Sustainable Income

Translating hobbies into sustainable revenue streams is not only an entrepreneurial venture; it is a method to combine one's passion with one's purpose in a society driven by the search for financial security. Individuals willing to reframe their hobbies as more than recreational pleasures are beginning to see the conventional wisdom of "do what you love, and you'll never work a day in your life" gradually transform into a realistic reality. This section aims to investigate the transforming path of turning interests into sustainable income. It explores the motivational roots, the practical actions needed, and the tremendous impact such a transition may have on personal fulfillment and financial well-being.

When it comes to turning hobbies into a source of income sustained over time, a fundamental adjustment in viewpoint is essential. It is a shift away from considering hobbies as nothing more than simple pleasures and toward acknowledging their inherent potential for economic viability. There are many different reasons why people decide to go on this path, but one thing unites them all: the desire to live a more purposeful and satisfying life. Many people feel tremendous fulfillment when they engage in activities they are passionate about, whether in art, crafts, writing, or any other hobby. Making money off these hobbies originates from the desire to match one's career with personal interests, resulting in a harmonious integration of one's life and professional environment.

Having a good knowledge of the marketable features of a pastime is the first step toward successfully converting it into a source of revenue that can be sustained over time. This requires an in-depth analysis of the attractiveness, one-of-a-kindness, and possible relevance of the interest to other people. As an illustration, a person who is enthusiastic about producing handcrafted items may investigate many paths, such as selling their wares on artisan platforms, taking part in craft fairs, or even holding seminars to share their expertise. When developing a feasible revenue plan, it is necessary to have a solid understanding of the market demand for particular components of the pastime.

In this day and age, personal branding has evolved into a powerful instrument for those interested in making money from their passions. Formulating a unique identity that strikes a chord with the intended audience is essential in developing a personal brand. This could be accomplished via consistent messaging, visual aesthetics, and a captivating story that emphasizes the knowledge and passion behind the occupation. Individuals can display their products, tell their narratives, and connect with a community of enthusiasts who share similar interests through social media, personal websites, and specialized markets.

One must change their thinking to transition from being a hobbyist to an entrepreneur. To successfully handle the hurdles and uncertainties inherent in developing a sustainable revenue stream, it is necessary to adopt an entrepreneurial mentality. Entrepreneurs are those who continually look for possibilities, innovate to satisfy the demands of the market, and demonstrate perseverance in the face of failure. Through applying this approach to turning interests into money, one must engage in strategic planning, establish goals, and demonstrate a willingness to adapt to the ever-changing dynamics of the market.

The transition from a pastime to a source of income is characterized by a series of actionable measures that change passion into profit. Included in these phases are fundamentally important is the execution of exhaustive market research. When placing the hobby within the market and determining its unique selling propositions, understanding the target demographic, the competitors, and the price dynamics is crucial.

To maintain a competitive advantage, engaging in ongoing improvement and skill growth is essential. Putting in the time and effort to improve one's abilities improves the overall quality of the activity and broadens the scope of the activities that may be enjoyed.

Developing a well-thought-out business strategy offers a road map for transforming a pastime into a source of revenue that can be maintained over time. Objectives, target markets, income sources, and marketing strategies are all outlined in this document.

Within the context of the current digital world, it is essential to have a robust online presence. Contributing to visibility and brand recognition includes activities such as developing a professional website, using social media platforms, and participating in online communities pertinent to the business.

Investigating different income streams relating to the pastime is beneficial to the hobby's stability and resilience. Among these options are the sale of items, the provision of services, the facilitation of workshops, and even the formation of partnerships with other artists.

As the pastime starts to generate cash, it is essential to have a comprehensive financial management strategy in place. To do this, you must create a budget, keep track of your spending, and reinvest your profits into expanding your hobby-turned-business.

The process of transforming interests into a sustainable income source can significantly influence one's sense of personal fulfillment, in addition to the financial ramifications. By bringing one's vocation into harmony with one's interests, one may cultivate a feeling of purpose and joy in the job that they are doing. In addition to the financial benefits, there is a sense of fulfillment that comes from sharing a passion dear to one's heart with a larger audience and receiving favorable comments. The route of turning interests into a sustainable income is characterized by a unique synergy formed by the twin advantage of financial stability and greater personal contentment (also known as "personal fulfillment").

The idea of converting interests into a source of revenue is appealing, but doing so only has its share of difficulties. Saturation of the market, intense rivalry, and the requirement to strike a balance between artistic expression and financial feasibility are all common obstacles. To overcome these obstacles, strategies include the following:

It is possible to differentiate oneself in a competitive market by concentrating on a specific subset of the hobby. The development of knowledge and the ability to appeal to a more specific target audience are made possible by specialization.

Through the establishment of relationships within the community and the formation of partnerships with other creators, new doors can be opened. Cross-promotion, the sharing of resources, and the collaborative problem-solving that may be accomplished through networking are all opportunities.

When operating in a dynamic market, it is essential to have a mindset that emphasizes continual innovation. Components crucial to continued success include the ability to adapt to evolving trends, the introduction of new products or services, and the solicitation of feedback for improvement.

Finding a way to honor one's artistic vision while still satisfying the market's requirements is a delicate act that requires careful consideration. Regular evaluations may maintain this equilibrium to see whether creative endeavors align with market trends.

Transforming one's interests into a source of income that can be maintained over time exemplifies the convergence of passion and practicality. It is a convincing demonstration of the transforming potential that may be achieved by bringing together economic viability and personal joy. In embarking on this entrepreneurship journey, individuals traverse a landscape where creativity and commerce collide, and passion becomes a driving force for achieving financially successful outcomes. Due to this paradigm shift, individuals are encouraged to reevaluate the borders that separate their personal interests and professional endeavors, which challenge old work and leisure opportunities concepts. Turning interests into sustainable income becomes a holistic undertaking, benefitting the individual and the community they participate in. This is because pursuing hobbies into sustainable income synthesizes passion and profit.

Building a Community Through Artisanal Skills

The concept of turning hobbies into a source of income sustained over time, characterized by shifting ideas on the relationship between labor and fulfillment, has gained remarkable significance in our period. There has been a movement in society, reflected in the concept of hobbies being recognized as possible economic pursuits rather than only being considered simple pleasures. This section delves into the dynamics of turning hobbies into sustainable income, exploring the motivations that are driving this trend, the diverse range of hobbies that can be monetized, the challenges that are being faced in this entrepreneurial pursuit, and the strategies that have been employed by individuals who have successfully converted their passions into viable and sustainable income streams.

Pursuing a more meaningful and satisfying way of life is at the core of transforming hobbies into a source of income that can be maintained over time. Many people start out on this path because they have a strong passion for the activity they have chosen, and they are looking for a way to combine their personal fun with their professional satisfaction. One of the strong motivators is the aspiration to break out of the humdrum of conventional jobs and build a career around something one enjoys doing. Individuals are motivated to investigate the possibility of turning their interests into a source of income because they seek autonomy, creative expression, and a more profound connection to their jobs.

A wide range of hobbies may be turned into a source of income, ranging from creative activities like painting, photography, and writing to more specialized interests like gardening, gaming, and crafting. The variety of hobbies that can be turned into a source of income is extensive and comprehensive. The proliferation of digital platforms has substantially expanded the range of options, making it possible for individuals to communicate with audiences worldwide using their one-of-a-kind abilities and creations. Hobbyists can now promote their work, network with other enthusiasts who share their interests, and, most importantly, make money from their skills or products thanks to the democratization of online spaces.

However, transforming interests into a source of income that can be sustained over time is challenging. In transitioning from a relaxed involvement with a pastime to adopting a formal business approach, one of the most significant challenges is the changeover. Those accustomed to the solely expressive character of their hobbies may need help managing the administrative components of their interests, such as marketing, financing, and customer relations. In addition, to successfully navigate the competitive environment and build a value offer that is one of a kind, one must be able to think strategically, be adaptable, and be aware of the market dynamics.

The development of a brand and establishing a presence on the internet are essential components for successfully monetizing hobbies in this era of digital technology. Establishing an easily identifiable brand requires establishing one's distinctive approach, voice, or style within the context of the chosen pastime. A comprehensive online presence helps reach a broader audience and attract new consumers or clients. This can be accomplished by displaying artwork on social media platforms, developing an e-commerce platform for handcrafted products, or creating a blog for posts that contain written material.

Effective marketing and networking are essential components to successfully transform interests into a source of income that can be sustained over time. Assisting in forming a supporting network may be accomplished through utilizing social media platforms, participating in relevant online forums, and attending events or fairs associated with the passion. Word-of-mouth, partnerships, and testimonials become extremely resourceful when increasing one's reach and building a reputation inside a specific specialty.

Successful people in this field frequently stress the significance of striking a balance between their passion and the business sustainability of their endeavors. The genuine delight that drove the interest in the first place may be diminished if it were transformed from a cherished passion into a simple job via the only consideration of money concerns. To achieve long-term success, it is essential to find a way to strike a delicate balance between preserving the essence of enjoyment and keeping alignment with financial feasibility.

One of the most essential strategies that people who have successfully monetized their hobbies have utilized is diversifying their existing money streams. This entails investigating the many different sources of money related to the pastime. As an illustration, a photographer could not only sell prints of their work but also provide photography seminars, license their photographs for use in commercial settings, or work together with other businesses. In addition to providing stability and boosting the endeavor's long-term sustainability, diversification helps offset the inherent risks involved with relying entirely on a single source of revenue.

Transforming hobbies into a source of income that can be maintained over time requires careful financial preparation. It is essential to have a solid understanding of the market demand, establish reasonable pricing, and create a budget for the firm's costs. In the context of this discussion, sustainability encompasses not just financial concerns but also the enterprise's influence on the environment and the individual. Maintaining a good work-life balance, adopting environmentally friendly practices, and employing manufacturing techniques that adhere to ethical standards are all factors that contribute to the long-term viability of the enterprise.

Case studies based on real-world examples of people who have successfully transformed their interests into sustainable income sources give significant insights and opportunities for inspiration. The examples above highlight the many tactics and strategies utilized across various interests. These examples range from independent artists selling their works on platforms like Etsy to content makers on YouTube or Twitch developing thriving communities. The examination of these trips provides valuable insights. It highlights the adaptation that is necessary in the quest to convert passions into enterprises that are not just profitable but also successful.

In conclusion, the transformation of hobbies into sources of revenue that can be sustained over time reflects a dynamic junction of passion and business. Individuals from a wide range of professions are investigating the great possibilities of monetizing their hobbies thanks to the desire to engage in work with a purpose and to have the freedom to express their creative side. Conquering obstacles, establishing a robust online presence, and diversifying sources of cash are all essential to achieving success in this effort. To secure the enterprise's long-term success, it is necessary to strike a balance between the company's passion and its commercial viability, in addition to engaging in smart financial planning. As a growing number of people begin on this path, the landscape of work and leisure continues to develop, hence offering chances for a new generation of hobbyists who have transitioned into entrepreneurs to succeed in the junction of their hobbies and professional endeavors.

CONCLUSION

Now that we have reached the end of our investigation into "Homestead Harmony: Off-Grid Projects for a Balanced Life," the trip into the realms of self-sufficiency, sustainability, and purposeful living takes the spotlight. This book serves as a guide, an inspiration, and a call to action for those looking to carve out a happy living off the main road in a world frequently dominated by fast-paced metropolitan lifestyles and internet connectedness. The spirit of the homesteading lifestyle, as depicted via a variety of projects and initiatives, goes beyond a simple rejection of conventional living; it contains an intense longing for a life that is balanced and purposeful because it is closely connected to nature, community, and the rhythm of the seasons.

The central concept that "Homestead Harmony" explores is the notion that creating, constructing, and surviving off the grid is not only a collection of projects but an approach to life that takes a holistic perspective. It is about accepting the challenge of constructing a life in harmony with one's values, aspirations for sustainability, and a desire for a more profound connection with the natural world. Each of the projects described in this book contributes to the overall storyline, providing readers with a toolset that will enable them to go on their own personal journey off the grid.

The knowledge that living off the grid is not a one-size-fits-all approach is one of the most essential things that can be removed from this investigation. Instead, it is a flexible and changeable lifestyle, and it can be adapted to fit a wide range of requirements, preferences, and external factors. The book provides a comprehensive roadmap for individuals to tailor their off-grid experience based on their unique aspirations and constraints.

It begins with establishing the groundwork for a sustainable homestead and then delves into specific projects such as solar power systems, rainwater harvesting, and environmentally friendly structures.

The notion of "balance" is woven throughout the fabric of this book, and it resonates in the decisions that individuals who have adopted the homesteading lifestyle have made. It is a balance between self-sufficiency and connectivity with community, between the conveniences of contemporary life and a return to living more simply and purposefully. Whether it's the sustainable energy solutions that strike a balance between technical development and environmental care or the artisanal skills that integrate traditional craftsmanship with current relevance, the different projects that have been highlighted serve as physical embodiments of this equilibrium.

Moreover, "Homestead Harmony" celebrates the

resiliency and flexibility of those who decide to live off the grid. It supports a mindset focused on problem-solving and continual development, and it accepts the problems that may come in this quest, both anticipated and unexpected. The tenacity homesteaders exhibit in the face of challenges, in conjunction with their dedication to continuous education and adoption of a Kaizen attitude, lends credence to the notion that the journey itself is just as significant as the goal.

In addition, the book highlights the connectivity of living

off the grid with more significant global concerns such as sustainability, environmental conscience, and responsible resource management. The off-grid initiatives shown here become more than just personal activities in our period, which is characterized by worries about climate change and a rising awareness of humans' influence on the globe. These projects become essential contributions to a more sustainable and peaceful world.

It is hoped that by the time readers reach the end of "Homestead Harmony," they will be prepared with information and practical skills and encouraged to start on their own off-grid journey. Those who want a life that vibrates with simplicity, purpose, and a profound connection to the natural world are the ones who are issued the invitation. Dreamers and doers alike are not excluded from this call. The projects described in this book are not only blueprints; they are catalysts for change that enable individuals to construct not only structures but also a life that is in accordance with their beliefs and goals.

The core of "Homestead Harmony" is that it encourages its readers to embrace the path of purposeful living, recognizing that it is a continuous process of discovery, adaptation, and development. The finale, which is harmonic and open-ended, reflects the ever-changing character of the farming lifestyle and the unending cycle of the seasons. May folks discover self-sufficiency and sustainability in their off-grid ventures and a profound feeling of fulfillment, community, and harmony with the planet around them as they begin their off-grid endeavors. According to the information presented in this book, the off-grid road is an invitation to embark on a life-altering journey that leads to a life that is not just constructed but also fashioned with intention, creativity, and a spirit that is in harmony.

Thank you for buying and reading/listening to our book. If you found this book useful/helpful please take a few minutes and leave a review on the platform where you purchased our book. Your feedback matters greatly to us.

www.ingramcontent.com/pod-product-compliance
Lightning Source LLC
Chambersburg PA
CBHW052053150726
48002CB00002B/872